We at Loyalty Savings hope
that this unique cookbook
will provide you and
your family with many
new insights into the
fascinating world of food.

Loyalty Savings
AND LOAN ASSOCIATION

Home Office: 5500 Folsom Boulevard, Sacramento 95819 . . . . (916) 452-6151
Arden Way Office: 2119 Arden Way, Sacramento 95813 . . . . (916) 925-3592
Citrus Heights Office: 7973 Auburn Boulevard, Citrus Heights 95610 . . . . . . (916) 967-8274
Florin Road Office: 6300 Florin Road, Sacramento 95822. . . . . (916) 421-6980
Rancho Cordova Office: 10134 Coloma Road, Rancho Cordova 95670 . . . . . (916) 362-1321

Lion from the avenue leading to the Ishtar gate of Babylon in the time of Nebuchadnezzar, Sixth Century B.C.

revised and enlarged

Cookbook of foods from Bible days

by Jean and Frank McKibbin

Illustrations and Recipes by Jean McKibbin
Layout by Sarah Gerdeman

COOKBOOK OF FOODS FROM BIBLE DAYS

Revised and enlarged

Printing History

Portions published in 1965 and 1966
as a newspaper feature column.
Selected columns published and copyright © 1966
as "Twelve Foods from the Bible."
Paperback edition COOKBOOK OF FOODS FROM BIBLE DAYS
published May 1971 by Voice Publications.

Revised and enlarged hard cover edition
published November 1972.

All rights reserved.

Copyright © 1972 by Frank L. McKibbin.
Portions copyright © 1965, 1966, 1971 by Frank L. McKibbin.

This book may not be reproduced
in whole or in part without permission.
For information address:
Frank L. McKibbin
6020 Wright Terrace
Culver City, California 90230

Printed in U.S.A.
Library of Congress catalog card number: 72-88527

Introduction

The concept of this book started over forty years ago with an interest in the Bible. But it took twenty years of experience in the food business and many years of fact gathering to bring it into being.

The area we define as the Near East has also been called the "fertile crescent" by Professor Breasted. It swings in a green arc from the Tigris-Euphrates valley in the east up through southern Turkey, down the Mediterranean coast to end in the Nile valley.

We began our studies with the earliest "high" civilization, the Sumerians in the Tigris-Euphrates valley. They left extensive references to crops, food, prices and medicine. Fortunately, they wrote on clay so their records have not perished.

Our studies broadened to Egypt, Palestine, Babylonia and other ancient countries that led finally to the great civilizations of Greece and Rome.

Then, one day my wife and I said in essence: "All this is most interesting; but it is essentially curiosa. How can we make it come alive and enjoy some of the experiences of these ancient people?" The answer was to try our hand at cooking this antique fare.

We found only two works on the subject written in this century. For those who would read further I recommend: "Plants of the Bible" by H. N. Moldenke and "The Roman Cookery Book" a translation of Apicius by Flower and Rosenbaum. Apicius wrote in Latin on cooking at the time of Tiberius, 42 B.C. to 37 A.D.

Outside these two sources we discovered we had to dig into archaeological reports, philological studies and others where, here and there, we would pick up a nugget of information about food in ancient times.

As we gathered information we checked the latest nutritional studies. It became evident that many of the ancient foods were highly nutritious. One is lead to ask: "If we accept that the 'fertile crescent' was chosen for man's development, is it not also likely the foods there might be especially conducive to man's physical, mental and even his spiritual well being?" We leave this to our readers to decide.

We believe you'll find the facts fascinating. We know you'll find the recipes good eating. Every one has been prepared lovingly at home and tasted with care.

F.McK.

dedicated to our children:
lynn, michael and mitch
who have endured uncomplainingly
our cooking and our counsel
for so many years.

jean and frank

contents

MEAT, FISH, FOWL

Brains	15
Fish	19
Goose	24
Kidneys	28
Lamb	32
Liver	37
Rabbit	41
Tuna	45

FRUITS, MELONS

Apples	51
Apricots	55
Carob	59
Dates	63
Figs	67
Grapes	71
Muskmelons	75
Olives	79
Pomegranates	83
Raisins	88
Watermelon	93

GRAIN, BREAD, NUTS

Almonds	99
Barley	103
Bread	107
Lentils	112
Walnuts	116
Wheat	120

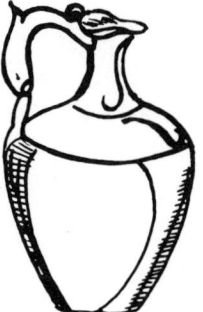

VEGETABLES

Artichokes	127
Beans	132
Cucumbers	136
Dandelion greens	140
Endive	144
Grape leaves	148
Green onions	152

DAIRY PRODUCTS

Butter	159
Cheese	164
Cottage cheese	168
Eggs	172
Milk	176
Yogurt	180

SWEETS, SPICE, SEASONING

Bay leaves	187
Cinnamon, cassia	191
Coriander	195
Cumin	199
Dill, anise, fennel	203
Garlic	207
Honey	211
Mint	215
Mustard	219
Olive oil	223
Salt	228
Sugarcane	233
Vinegar	238
Wine	243

INDEX 247

meat, fish, fowl

In the Royal Cemetery at Ur in ancient Sumeria was unearthed a lyre. This bull's head was the ornament for the sound-box. The art is done in gold and lapis lazuli. Circa 2500 B.C.

BRAINS

Since meat was eaten much less frequently in the ancient world than we do today it was natural for every part of the animal to be consumed. Archaeological "digs" often turn up piles of bones that have been opened carefully to get out the marrow.

Consequently the brains of animals have constituted an important part of mankind's fare for thousands of years. Recipes for them have come down to us from antiquity using them for an ingredient as well as cooked for themselves. Among primitive people there is a belief that eating certain animals or certain parts will give the eater the characteristics possessed by that animal or part. This is called sympathetic or homoeopathic magic. Thus a primitive man might feel that when he ate the heart or brain of an animal he took on its bravery or wisdom. Remnants of this kind of belief exist even today in this country among some individuals. For them eating brains would mean they were acquiring added mental power.

Though this belief is no longer widely held we do know that brains, and other variety meats like kidney, sweetbreads, liver and heart are unusually rich in minerals and vitamins. Brains, for instance, have over twice as much phosphorus as T-bone steak, four times as much vitamin B_1. In fact, brains are an excellent source of several members of the vitamin B complex like B_1, B_2 (riboflavin) and cholin which is not strictly speaking a vitamin but is included in the B complex family.

The Roman chef Apicius of the first century A.D. mixed brains with seafood, rabbit, chicken, peas, wheat and a number of other foods. The Hebrew New Year is called Rosh Hashana which literally means "head of the year." To symbolize this meaning Jews in some countries serve a sheep or fish head at their New Year's meal. In Greece they sometimes serve "pestelles" filled with lamb or other brains for the same symbolic reason.

Brains are a gourmet dish. In flavor they are rich as butter even though they do not contain as much fat as a comparable amount of choice T-bone steak. Whether you buy beef, veal, calf, lamb or pork brains you will find the flavor delicate and the texture very tender. So they are interchangeable. Brains are highly perishable and should be cooked as soon as possible after purchase. If you buy them frozen be sure to keep them frozen until you're ready to use them. Then cover with hot water. Let set until they are just barely thawed, and proceed with their preparation. If you buy them fresh be sure to keep them refrigerated but try not to store them more than 24 hours.

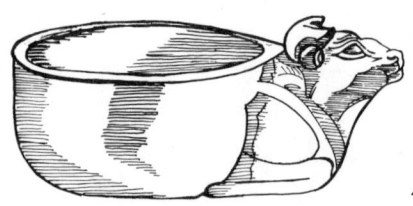

A wild ox head decorates this ancient bowl.

TO PREPARE BRAINS wash in cold water, then soak 1 hour in a quart of water to which you add 1 tbs. salt. Remove the membrane with tip of a knife. Drop into boiling water to which you add 1 tsp. salt and 1 tbs. vinegar per quart. Simmer 20 minutes. If you cook them longer you spoil the texture. Drain. Rinse and soak 15 minutes in cold water. Drain again. Thus prepared they're ready for the following recipes.

BRAINS FRIED (A Greek Recipe)

    2 calves' brains
    3 tsp. salt
      oil for frying
    2 tbs. flour
    1 egg, beaten
      pepper
      cracker meal

Prepare brains as outlined in preceding paragraph. Then cut in ½ inch slices, roll in flour, dip in beaten egg, salt and pepper. Roll in cracker meal. Fry in oil until golden brown on both sides.

BRAINS WITH SCRAMBLED EGGS

    1 cup brains (prepared as outlined above)
    1 tbs. butter or margarine
    3 eggs
    3 tbs. cream
    ⅛ tsp. salt
      pepper

Fry brains in butter until brown. Beat the eggs, cream, salt and dash of pepper and add to the brains. Cook over low heat. As the eggs begin to thicken stir lightly with a fork. When thick, serve on a slice of hot buttered toast.

For an unbelievably different dish, and one that will surprise you with a unique and delicate taste, the following is highly recommended. Serve it with pieces of Bedouin Bread as an hors d'oeuvre and watch your guests, who wouldn't eat brains on a bet, tasting it again and again with puzzled pleasure.

APICIUS' APPETIZER

4 lamb brains (prepared as outlined above)
1 tbs. onion, minced
2 cloves garlic, crushed
½ cup lemon juice
1 tbs. parsley, minced
salt and pepper to taste

Mix onion, garlic, lemon juice and parsley. Pour over diced brains. Season to taste and refrigerate. Drain off excess juice and serve cold.

BAKED BRAINS WITH EGG

2 cups brains (prepared as outlined above)
2 tomatoes, peeled and diced
2 tbs. olive oil
1 tbs. parsley, minced
1 tbs. onion, minced
1 tsp. brown sugar
salt and pepper
4 eggs
3 tbs. butter or margarine
3 tsp. lemon juice

Place brains in 4 buttered individual casseroles. Mix tomatoes, olive oil, parsley, onion, brown sugar, salt and pepper. Pour over brains. Break 1 egg carefully into each dish. Bake at 350° 10 minutes, or until egg is firm. Brown the butter in a small skillet, add lemon juice and pour over. Serve hot.

fish

Man carrying fish. From the Standard of Ur, a wooden panel inlaid with shell and lapis lazuli. Found in a grave in the ancient city of Ur. Circa 2500 B.C.

Among the annals of antiquity and in illustrations found by archaeologists fish references are so numerous they would fill a book.

Out of the mists of pre-historic times from the dwellings of stone age men come fish bones and fishing implements. At a dwelling site called Nea Nikomedeia on the Greek mainland (near modern Thessalonika) have been found piles of fish bones and shells of fresh and salt water shellfish. Searchers of caves and rock shelters in Mesopotamia have come across fish bones dated long before the dawn of history.

When the curtain rose on ancient man with his first written records we are presented with a vast storehouse of facts about fish in the everyday life and the religion of many different peoples. The Sumerians of 4,000 to 6,000

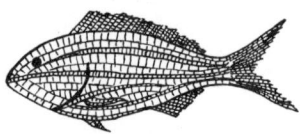

years ago, in the Tigris-Euphrates valley, believed that their god Enki had given them fish as a special gift. So important was this food that the piety of their kings was measured by the supply of fish they provided in sacrifices to the gods.

A Sumerian proverb (after Gordon) gives a delightful insight into domestic life. In it a wife speaks of the ideal marriage: "And let my husband remove the bones from the fish for me." Other Sumerian records speak of 100 fishermen attached to a single temple. Over 50 kinds of fish are mentioned in these texts and several kinds of fishermen: river, canal, coast and high seas.

Sumerian writers also speak of fish ponds. Other finds give us a rather surprising picture of the widespread use of private ponds for fish raising. In Isaiah 19:10 the Bible refers to the Egyptian practice of keeping fish ponds. This reference is given historical support by the oldest known illustration of a private pond. It is a 4,000 year old bas-relief in the tomb of an Egyptian gentleman. So good is the delineation of the fish he is pulling from the pond that they can be identified as Tilapia, a relative of the common North American sunfish. In Israel Tilapia are common even today in the Sea of Galilee where they frequently are called "St. Peter's Fish."

The Bible abounds with references to fish and fishermen. In the very first chapter the Lord gives man dominion over the fish of the sea. (Genesis 1:26 and 28) As the children of Israel wandered in the wilderness one of the foods they longed for were fish which they ate so freely in Egypt. (Numbers 11:5) The New Testament tells many stories that connect Jesus with fish. When he appeared before his disciples after resurrection they gave him a piece of broiled fish. (Luke 24:42) He fed the multitude with bread and fish. (Matthew 14:17,18,19) Early Christians used the fish as a symbol because the letters of its name, ICHTHUS in Greek, were the first letters of the phrase: "Jesus Christ, Son of God, Savior."

Whether you're observing Lent or are interested simply in good fish here are three recipes we recommend. We've used methods of cooking that were common in ancient times, broiling, baking and simmering in sauce.

FISH OF GALILEE

"As soon then as they were come to land, they saw a fire of coals there, and fish laid thereon, and bread." John 21:9

> 6 small trout
> 3 onions, sliced
> ½ cup cooking oil
> ½ tsp. coriander, ground
> parsley
> salt and pepper
> juice of 1 lemon

On barbecue grill brush some cooking oil. To remaining oil add coriander and brush fish inside and out. Place onion slices and a sprig of parsley in the cavities. Salt and pepper fish. Broil over hot coals of barbecue. Add lemon juice to balance of oil mixture for basting fish. Brown fish well before turning. Time: about 15 minutes.

Ancient Roman mosaic now in Museum of Antiquities in Tripoli shows lobster, a Parrotfish (also called Porgy) and a red mullet.

BAKED FISH

2 lbs. fish filets
½ cup butter or margarine
1 small onion, chopped
½ cup milk
salt and pepper

Place filets in oven-proof dish. Dot generously with butter and sprinkle onions over them. Add milk and seasonings. Bake at 350 degrees until done, about 20 minutes. Garnish with chopped parsley and serve with lemon wedges. Makes 4 servings.

Ancient fishermen equipped with nets and spears probably had the same sort of luck as their modern counterparts. A catch of small fish could be cooked over an open fire. A large fish could be baked in a clay oven. But when the catch was a miscellany of small and large a different solution was required. It is quite probable the cooking pot was the answer. Odds and ends of available foods were combined to give birth to a fish stew or chowder. A tasty, modern version of this ancient meal follows.

SIMON PETER FISH STEW

(See Luke 5:6 and John 21:6)

2 lb. any firm fish filet, cut in 1 inch cubes
8 slices bacon, cut up
2 onions, chopped
1 14½ oz. can peeled tomatoes
1 8 oz. can tomato sauce
3 potatoes, peeled and cubed
1 or 2 tbs. Worcestershire sauce
   (depending on your taste)
2 tsp. salt
½ tsp. pepper
chopped parsley to garnish

Sauté bacon in large, heavy pan. Add onion and cook until tender. Quarter and remove stem end from tomatoes. Add all ingredients except fish. Simmer, stirring occasionally, for 20 to 25 minutes, until potatoes are almost done. Add fish and let simmer for 5 to 10 minutes until potatoes are tender and fish flakes easily. Serve in bowls with parsley garnish. Serves 6.

GOOSE

From the fifth century B.C. a goose on the base of a cup unearthed in Athens, Greece.

The Bible does not mention geese by name. But from other sources we know they have been eaten in Bible lands for thousands of years.

Certainly geese would have been one of the fowls that Noah released from the Ark. "And every beast, every creeping thing and every bird, . . . went forth by families out of the ark." Gen. 8:19 (RSV) We are certain that geese were included in the statement in Deuteronomy 14:11 (RSV): "You may eat all clean birds." For in 1970 B.C. an Egyptian exile named Sinuhe left a record of how kind the people of northern Palestine were to him. They served him bread and wine and roast goose.

Pictures in Egyptian tombs nearly 5,000 years old tell us that geese were relished then. In fact, the Egyptians believed that even to dream of killing a goose was a good omen. By Roman times geese were an important dish in banquets given by royalty. The Roman poet Horace describes the utter deliciousness of the liver of a goose that had been fattened on ripe figs. In Yugoslavia and neighboring countries geese are still specially fattened to enlarge their livers for production of paté de fois gras. Their feet are nailed to a board so they cannot move. They are then force fed to make their livers grow to two and three times normal size.

One of the oldest cook books we have is written in Latin by the famous chef Apicius at the time of Christ. In it he gives recipes for cooking ostrich, cranes, turtle-doves, thrush, peacock, pheasant and, of course, goose. Before turkey was introduced to Europe from the New World goose was the traditional Christmas bird in many countries. It has remained traditional to this day for a multitude of families in both Europe and America.

Geese are at their best in fall and winter months which may be one reason for their popularity at Christmas. Another, of course, is that they are the richest eating of all domestic birds. Goose has less water and more fat than chicken, turkey or even duck. In merry Old England aristocrats sometimes dined on swan and peacock but goose was the honored Christmas bird for most of the people. It is a special treat for lovers of dark meat since it has no white meat at all.

Goose was immortalized by Dickens in his heart warming description of the Cratchit's Christmas dinner. "Bob said he didn't believe there ever was such a goose cooked. Its tenderness and flavor, size and cheapness were the themes of universal admiration."

ROAST GOOSE

1 young (8 to 12 lb.) goose
2 tsp. salt
1 tsp. pepper
1 tsp. ground ginger

Cover neck, heart and gizzard with salted water. Simmer 1 hour to make stock for dressing and gravy. Wash goose carefully. Remove as much fat as possible and save. Dry goose and rub inside and out with salt, pepper and ginger. Fill goose with dressing. Do not pack tight since dressing swells. Sew up all openings. Roast on rack in uncovered pan at 325 degrees. Allow 30 minutes per pound.

Render the fat over low heat and save for cooking. Goose fat is so rich it can be used in place of butter for sautéing or as shortening in your pastries.

For gravy pour all fat out of pan except for about ¼ cup. Leave this in the pan in which the goose has been roasted. Blend in 4 tbs. flour. Then slowly stir in 2 cups of stock. Continue to cook and stir until it is smooth and has boiled 1 minute to thicken. Season to taste.

Drawing of a Phrygian painted vessel unearthed at Gordium in the "Child's Tumulus." The Phrygians drove the Hittites from their kingdom in the 8th and 9th centuries B.C.

DRESSING

- 3 cups diced dry bread
- 2 cups apples, peeled, cored and diced
- 1 cup prunes, cooked and cut up
- ¾ cup chopped celery
- ½ cup chopped walnuts
- ½ cup stock (made as noted above)
- salt and pepper to taste

Combine ingredients and stuff the bird lightly as instructed above.

For a treat with dinner soak the goose liver for 2 hours in cold, salted water. Dry and sauté until tender in goose fat. Season with salt, pepper and ginger. Add 1 tbs. water, cover and simmer for 5 minutes. Cut in bite size pieces and serve on toothpicks as hors d'oeuvres.

For a delectable accompaniment to this meal serve glazed apricots. The recipe is in the chapter on apricots. After you have dined on the goose, any meat remaining can be used in the same way that you would prepare leftover chicken. Creamed, soufflé, curry or aspic salads are all good. Here is a salad that is easy to make and excellent eating.

SINUHE SALAD

Quantities depend on how much goose you have.
diced cooked goose
hearts of celery, chopped
green onions, chopped
canned or fresh cooked peas
stuffed olives, sliced
gherkin pickles, sliced
mayonnaise
cream

Mix a little cream with mayonnaise to thin it slightly. Toss all ingredients together and refrigerate. Serve on a bed of crisp lettuce.

kidneys

Saqqara was an important locale during the early Dynastic Period of Egypt. There King Djoser built the oldest pyramid yet discovered, the famous Step Pyramid, during his reign from circa 2778 to 2723 B.C. The scene shown here is from a tomb in Saqqara. It shows cattle passing a canal.

The seat of our emotions, of love, hate and fear, we think of figuratively as being in the heart; but for the people of Bible days it was the kidneys. These ancient people believed the heart was the seat of thought.

Thus, in the King James version of the Bible we read: "Examine me, O Lord, and prove me; try my *reins* and my heart." (Psalms 26:2) "Reins" was the word for kidneys used at the time of this translation. It is derived from the Latin "renes" which means kidneys. This same passage in the recent Revised Standard Version of the Bible is rendered: "Prove me, O Lord, and try me; test my heart and my mind."

The Rabbinical teachings of the Talmud, that ancient set of laws that dates back before the time of Christ, reflect the belief that kidneys are the seat of man's emotions. In one passage the Talmud states that of man's two kidneys one prompts him to do good and the other to do evil.

Knowing these facts it is easy to understand why the people of Bible times regarded kidneys so highly. Since they were considered one of the most important parts of the body as well as delectable they were called for in sacrifices to the Lord. (Exodus 29:13; Leviticus 3:4)

Kidneys have been eaten as a delicacy for thousands of years; but today they are eaten simply as food with no emotional connotation. If you have never tried them you are missing a truly delicious food. The French and other experienced European gourmets serve them as a particularly dainty dish fit for kings and lovers of good food. Yet, like most variety meats, kidneys are usually inexpensive. And they have a particular importance in our diet. Just as liver, heart and sweetbreads they contain more nutrients than the muscle-meats we ordinarily eat. Kidneys are a far richer source of minerals and various vitamins than the finest T-bone steak. For instance, they contain nearly 10 times as much vitamin A as T-bone, although liver has even more. They're higher in vitamin B_1 than liver and second only to the latter in treating anemia.

The best eating kidneys come from beef, lamb and veal. Pork kidneys are usually lower in cost but less frequently found at the meat counter. Beef kidneys weigh about a pound, veal five to twelve ounces and lamb around two ounces. If your family isn't too high on liver by all means try them on kidneys. You'll be doing your budget and your family's nutrition a big favor. Most important, you'll be adding an especially delicious food to your menus.

We personally have a special place in our cooking for veal kidney chops which are chops with a sweet, delectable morsel of kidney in them. At fine meat markets you'll find them separate and probably a bit higher in price than the usual chops. Otherwise you may have to ask your butcher to pick them out of the regular pile of chops.

VEAL KIDNEY CHOPS

Dip chops in beaten egg, then in fine bread crumbs. Brown both sides in butter or margarine in heavy pan. Add about half cup water, salt and pepper. Cover. Simmer for 30 minutes, checking once in awhile to be sure they are not sticking. Add a little more water if needed. Turn and simmer 15 minutes more. All juice should be used up in the cooking and chops should be golden brown and very tender.

KINGLY KIDNEYS

1 lb. lamb kidneys (about 8)
6 tbs. butter or margarine
¼ lb. mushrooms, sliced (a 4 oz. can will do)
1 tbs. onion, minced
1 tbs. parsley, minced
1 clove garlic, crushed
salt and pepper
½ cup sour cream

Soak kidneys in salted water half an hour. Rinse. Cut in half and remove white core. Slice very thin. Melt 2 tbs. butter in heavy pan and brown mushrooms lightly about 5 minutes. Remove and keep them warm. Add remaining butter to pan with kidneys, onion, parsley and seasonings. Stir over high heat until browned, about 8 minutes. Add garlic and mushrooms. Reduce heat. Let simmer about 5 minutes. Add sour cream and stir until blended and hot. Serve over rice. Serves 6.

BROILED KIDNEYS WITH GARLIC

(to increase or decrease amount
allow 2 kidneys for each serving)

8 lamb kidneys
1 small bay leaf
1 lemon, sliced thin
2 tbs. butter or margarine
1 or 2 cloves garlic, crushed
salt and pepper

Wash the kidneys in cold water. Split in two lengthwise. Remove fat and white veins with a sharp pointed knife or manicure scissors. Place bay leaf in a sauce pan and cover bottom of the pan with lemon slices. Place kidneys over the lemon. Add remaining lemon slices on top. Pour in 1 cup of water and boil gently for 10 to 15 minutes, until tender. Melt the butter in a small saucepan while kidneys cook. Add seasoning and garlic and let it bubble for a minute, then set aside. Drain the kidneys, dip them in the garlic sauce and arrange on the broiler rack. Broil 3 inches from heat source, 3 minutes on one side and 2 to 3 minutes on the other.

Serve hot on a bed of rice. Spoon remaining garlic sauce over them.

LAMB

*Relief from a stone vase circa 3500 B.C.
Found in the ruins of the city called Erech in the Bible.
It is located about 180 miles northwest of the head
of the Persian Gulf near the Euphrates.*

Lamb is associated with important religious days for both Christians and Jews. For Christians it is one of the traditional meats at Easter.

Jews eat lamb on Seder evenings, the first and second nights of Passover. For the Jews it symbolizes the story in Exodus 12 when God spared the lives of their firstborn by passing over the homes where the blood of the lamb had been sprinkled on the doorposts.

The lamb as an animal was so highly thought of in

Bible days that John referred to Jesus as a lamb: "and he looked at Jesus as he walked and said, 'Behold the Lamb of God!'"

Outside of its religious associations lamb has been an important meat at all seasons of the year. Certainly one of the most familiar scenes described in the Old and New Testaments is that of the shepherd and his flock. In fact, the shepherd's crook was so characteristic of the nomads that the Egyptians used it as the sign in their picture writing to designate these foreigners.

Both the Bible and archaeological excavations show abundant evidence of the wide use of sheep for food. The popularity of lamb throughout the entire Near East is attested by the multitude of recipes that have come down to us. The Greeks, Syrians, Turks and others, as well as the Hebrews, prepare every edible part of a lamb in a wide variety of ways. In Syria during the feasting season families buy a whole lamb. It is then fattened for a week on mulberry leaves and malt, dressed, rubbed with spices and barbecued on a spit over a bed of coals.

In recognition of both Christian and Jewish custom in serving lamb at Easter and Passover we offer below recipes for each of these faiths. In Exodus 12:8 (RSV) the Jews are told exactly how to prepare the Passover lamb: "... eat the flesh ... roasted; with unleavened bread and bitter herbs." Only unleavened bread may be eaten during the 7 days of the festival in memory of the fact that the Jews hastening from Egypt had no time to leaven their bread.

Overcooking lamb makes it leathery and grayish brown. Cook until it is a faint pink. Then it is mild flavored, juicy and tender. Broiling and roasting are most often used for lamb since it is always tender and juicy. Inasmuch as wine in moderation is approved in the Bible (See Psalms 104:15; I Timothy 5:23) we give you a superb recipe for:

ROAST LEG OF LAMB WITH WINE

    1 leg of lamb (5 to 6 lb.)
    2 cups dry, white wine
    2 tbs. cooking oil
    1 clove garlic, crushed
    ¼ tsp. each of: rosemary, thyme, marjoram, oregano and fresh or dried crushed mint leaf
    2 tbs. butter or margarine
    ½ cup walnuts, chopped
    5 chicken livers
    1 can mushrooms (4 oz.)
    3 tbs. flour
    1½ cups water
    salt and pepper to taste

Place lamb in a bowl. Prepare a marinade by mixing wine with the garlic, herbs and oil. Pour this over lamb and set aside for at least 4 hours, or overnight, if possible. Turn a few times or spoon marinade over meat. When ready to cook place lamb, fat side up, on a rack in a shallow roasting pan. Leave uncovered and roast in oven at 325 degrees for 2½ to 3 hours. Approximately 35 min. per pound gives you medium cooked lamb; 40 min. for well-done. Meat thermometer readings: medium—175 degrees; well—182. Baste often with marinade.

  Meanwhile toast walnuts in butter in small pan. Remove and set aside. Cook chicken livers in same pan until done and cut into small pieces. Mix livers, nuts and mushrooms with their liquid plus any remaining marinade. Simmer about 5 minutes. When roast is done place on platter. Skim excess fat from drippings in pan and add water. Stir and cook until drippings dissolve. Add liver-nut-mushroom mixture. Mix flour with a little water and add to other ingredients. Cook and stir until the sauce thickens. Season with salt and pepper. To serve, carve lamb and pour hot sauce over the slices.

PASSOVER LAMB

1 shoulder of lamb
garlic cloves
rosemary
salt and pepper

Make small slits in roast and insert 4 to 12 garlic cloves depending on your taste for garlic. Sprinkle with rosemary, salt and pepper. Put roast, uncovered, in a hot oven (450 degrees) for half hour. Then reduce heat to 300 degrees. Continue roasting until done (see recipe instructions above). If meat is very lean you may brush with oil a few times while roasting.

Judges 6:19 (RSV) tells us ". . . Gideon went into his house and prepared a kid, and unleavened cakes from an ephah of flour. . . ." The same combination of foods is included in this easy and attractive "dinner in a dish" recipe for lamb. It's good any time of year. When served with a salad it makes a complete meal.

LAMB SKILLET PIE

    1 lb. ground lamb
    1 large onion, chopped
    1 or 2 ribs celery, chopped
    ½ green pepper, chopped
    1 8 oz. can tomato sauce
    1 8 oz. can mushrooms, drained
    ½ tsp. salt
    ¼ tsp. pepper

Brown lamb lightly in heavy skillet. Add onion, celery and green pepper. Cook until onion is lightly golden and transparent. Drain off excess fat and add remaining ingredients. Mix well. Then firm down in the skillet with a spatula.

BATTER

Sift together:
    ½ cup corn meal
    ½ cup flour
    1 tsp. baking powder
    ½ tsp. salt
Beat together:
    ⅓ cup shortening
    ½ cup milk
    1 egg
    1 tbs. minced parsley
    ½ tsp. celery seed

Combine the two and mix. Then spoon over the meat mixture. Bake at 400 degrees for about 20 minutes—until crust is golden brown. Remove from oven and let stand 10 to 15 minutes to absorb juice and firm up. Slip a knife around edge to loosen crust from pan. Place a serving dish upside down over pan and quickly invert. Cut in wedges to serve. Serves 6.

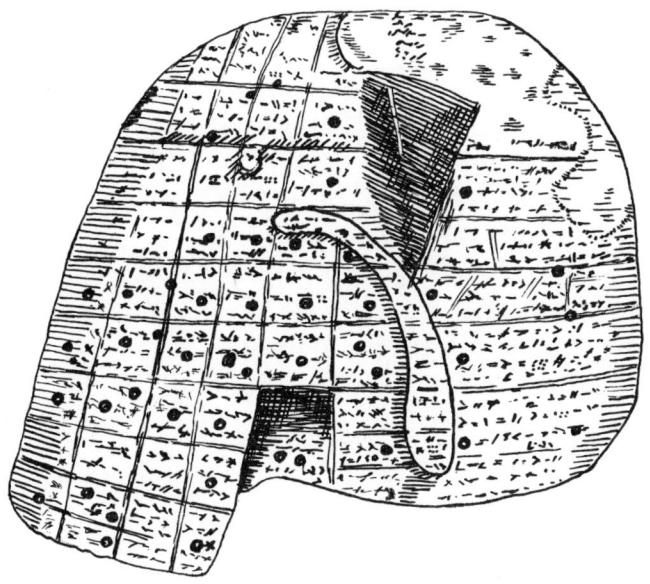

The Babylonians, among others, believed in soothsaying by "reading" animal livers. Divination by examining livers is known as hepatoscopy. The model shown here is that of a sheep made in clay with inscriptions showing how it is "read." 19th century B.C.

LIVER

Animal livers played a remarkably important role in the lives of the people of the ancient Near East.

For the Babylonians of the second millenium B.C. and the Hittites who followed them in Asia Minor the liver was essential to foretelling the future. This art of "divination" depended on diviner-priests who slaughtered an animal—usually a sheep—and read the signs they found on its liver. This practice was based on the belief that the gods sent signs to their followers by marking the liver of an animal to be sacrificed.

Clay models of livers have been found in Mesopotamia and Asia Minor. These models were marked with holes and lines that were regarded as significant and coded with cuneiform words to indicate the meaning of each sign. The Etruscans who preceded the Romans in Italy made bronze models of livers with similar markings and interpretive coding. If a king was preparing to go into battle, make an important decision or seeking the cause of the wrath of a god he would call in his special priests to read a liver. See illustration.

Ezekiel 21:21 tells of a king of Babylon who "looked in a liver." So it is evident that the people of Bible times were fully conversant with the reading of livers. But more important than this to the followers of our Bible, the liver was considered a delicacy. Along with fat and other prime parts of an animal it was used as a sacrifice to the Lord. (Exodus 29:13; Leviticus 3:4, etc.)

A startling contrast to the belief in divination is an ancient down-to-earth prescription of liver to cure night blindness and related eye symptoms. This advice was contained in medical texts found in Egyptian tombs dating around 1900 B.C. Four thousand years later modern science has confirmed that night blindness can be treated with doses of vitamin A in which liver is quite rich. Unlike the muscle meats such as roasts, chops, steaks and so on liver contains both vitamins A and C. For instance, just 3½ ounces of fried beef liver can contain 53,400 units of vitamin A whereas the same amount of T-bone steak has 80.

In addition to vitamins A and C all kinds of liver, whether from beef, pork, lamb or calf, are excellent sources of good-quality protein, iron, riboflavin and niacin. The amount of vitamin A increases with age. For this reason liver from mature beef or sheep is richer in this vitamin than that from younger animals like calf and lamb. However, the liver from the latter is preferred for its milder flavor and tenderness.

Here's a dish fit for any king:

PATRICIAN PATÉ

1 lb. chicken livers
½ lb. chicken fat
1 large onion
½ stick butter or margarine
1 cup milk
¼ cup flour
2 eggs
1 tsp. salt
¼ tsp. pepper

Put livers, fat and onion through a food grinder twice using the finest blade. Melt butter or margarine in sauce pan. Add flour and slowly stir in milk to make a white sauce. Add to liver mixture and stir well. Beat eggs and seasoning and stir into liver mixture. Bake in a buttered dish set in a pan of water at 350 degrees for one hour, then 400 degrees for another 30 minutes. Serve as hors d'oeuvres with crackers at your next party and watch it go.

This recipe is a welcome variation from the usual fried liver. If vinegar with liver sounds "far out" you'll be surprised to find how delicately flavored it is. The strong scent of vinegar is all in the steam.

LIVER VINAIGRETTE

1 lb. calf liver, sliced thin
½ lb. fresh mushrooms
6 tbs. butter or margarine
¼ cup vinegar, preferably wine vinegar
1 clove garlic, crushed

Melt 1 tbs. butter or margarine in heavy sauce pan. Sauté liver quickly. Brown both sides but it should still be pink inside. Place on a platter and keep hot. Sauté mushrooms lightly in same pan. Spoon over liver. Add remaining butter to pan drippings with vinegar and garlic. Bring to fast boil. Pour over liver. Serves 4.

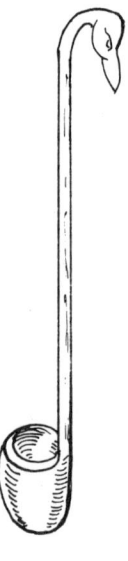

Both ancient and modern cooking instructions from all of the Mediterranean countries contain many recipes for cooking liver. One of our favorite recipes is of Arabic origin. Originally the mint and garlic were probably used to mask the flavor of liver from an old animal, but even with the tasty, tender liver of veal the following combination is excellent.

LIVER BROILED WITH GARLIC SAUCE

2 lb. veal or beef liver   1 tsp. salt
2 to 3 cloves garlic, crushed   1 tbs. olive oil
10 to 12 mint leaves   coarse pepper

Crush garlic, mint, salt and pepper together. Mix in the olive oil. Spread over slices of liver. Cover and let stand for 30 minutes to an hour. Broil about 3 inches from heat source 4 to 5 minutes each side, or pan fry in butter. Cook until firm but still faintly pink for best flavor. Serves 4 to 6.

RABBIT

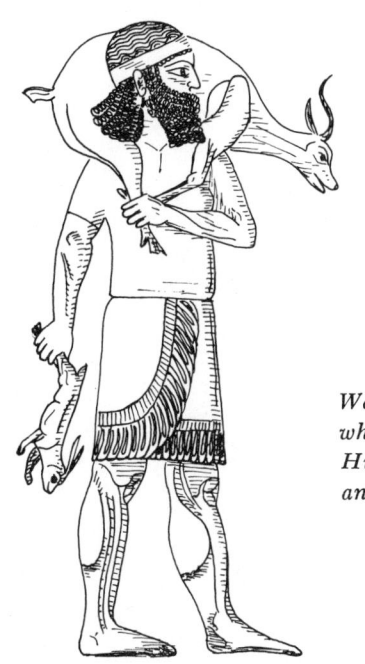

Wall relief from Khorsabad where Sargon II built his capital in 8th century B.C. Hunter returns with a small deer over his shoulders and a hare in his right hand.

Favorite game of hunters from the Stone Age to the Twentieth Century—that's our prolific little rabbit.

As recently as 1965 excavators at the site of Nea Nikomedeia in northern Greece (it lies near modern day Thessalonika) found rabbit bones in the remains of campfires. They are at least 8,000 years old. All over the Mediterranean, from the island of Crete in prehistoric times to ancient Egypt, rabbit bones have been found with unmistakable evidence they were used for food. Before the domestication of animals it is quite evident that rabbits were an important source of food. In the 9,500 year old ruins of a village in Syria, called Tell Mureybat, beside the Euphrates only the bones of *wild* animals have been found. This means that domestic animals were not yet kept for food. Rabbit bones form a good percentage of this find.

As we come into historic times we find some charming hunting scenes that portray our familiar bunny quite clearly. A color rendering from an Egyptian tomb of the 18th Dynasty (1537 to 1320 B.C.) shows a slave carrying a large panier of ostrich eggs in one hand and a long-eared rabbit in the other. See illustration in chapter on eggs. From ancient Khorsabad in Iraq around the time of Sargon II (8th century B.C.) we have another scene of hunters, one of whom carries a hare in addition to other game he has shot as shown in the illustration.

By Roman times hares were popular food. The agriculturist Varro in the first century B.C. gives detailed descriptions for keeping rabbits in warrens and fattening them for the table in hutches. His near-contemporary, the chef Apicius, has thirteen recipes for cooking rabbit.

Despite the obvious relish with which most people of Bible days ate rabbit the Jews were forbidden to do so. "And the hare, because he cheweth the cud, but divideth not the hoof; he is unclean unto you." (Leviticus 11:6) This was the law as laid down by Moses. Actually, the rabbit does not chew the cud, but the action of his mouth is such that it appears he does.

The distinction between a rabbit and a hare is slight. True hares have longer ears and hind legs than rabbits. Our jack rabbit and the snowshoe rabbit of the north are hares. The domesticated rabbits of the U.S. are varieties developed from European strains which, in turn, are native to the western Mediterranean.

Rabbits are excellent eating. If you shoot your own in the colder months you'll find a gamey flavor and probably a piece or two of unexpected buckshot. But domesticated rabbit has become increasingly available on the market. It is all government inspected. Like other lean meats, poultry and lean fish, rabbit is a good source of high quality proteins. It is fine-grained, mild-flavored and practically all white meat. Rabbit is cooked and eaten just like chicken.

"Fryers" are 8 to 12 weeks old; "roasters" are usually 8 months or older and can weigh well over 4 pounds. Small, young rabbits may be fried or stewed. But the larger fryers and roasters need long, slow cooking in a covered pan to make sure they are tender.

The following recipe for rabbit in a wine sauce is excellent. As a "cook ahead" dish it's even better. It can be cooked a day ahead of time and refrigerated, then heated while you cook the rice. When serving, catch a few of the raisins in the spoon as you ladle the sauce over the rice.

RABBIT IN WINE SAUCE

   3 pound rabbit fryer, cut in serving pieces
  ¼ cup olive oil
  ½ tsp. salt
     pepper
   1 cup dry wine
   1 tbs. sugar
   1 tbs. wine vinegar
   3 cloves garlic, crushed
   1 8 oz. can tomato sauce
  ⅛ to ¼ tsp. cayenne (depending on your taste)
   2 tbs. parsley, chopped fine
   3 tbs. raisins

Wash the rabbit parts and dry with paper towels. Heat olive oil in a heavy skillet and fry the rabbit until well browned. Season with salt and pepper. Lower heat. Mix remaining ingredients and pour over the rabbit. Cover. Simmer for an hour, turning and basting occasionally. When tender remove rabbit to a platter. Thicken the sauce with a little flour. Serve with rice over which the sauce is ladled like a gravy. Serves 4 to 6.

OVEN FRIED RABBIT

1 fryer rabbit, 2½ to 3 lb. cut up
½ cup flour
1 tsp. salt
¼ tsp. pepper
½ tsp. paprika
butter or margarine for browning

Mix all dry ingredients in a paper bag. Put in rabbit pieces and shake well. Heat butter in skillet and brown rabbit on both sides. Place browned pieces on broiler rack in medium oven—350 degrees. Cook about an hour or until very tender. Serves 4.

RABBIT FRICASSEE

1 rabbit, about 3 lb. cut into serving pieces ready to cook
salt, pepper
flour for dredging
4 tbs. butter, margarine or oil for browning
2 cups hot water or stock
¼ cup chopped onions
2 sprigs parsley
1 or 2 ribs celery

Season rabbit with salt and pepper. Dredge with flour. Heat butter or oil in heavy skillet and sauté rabbit until lightly browned. Add remaining ingredients. Cover. Let simmer, but do not boil, until meat is tender—about one hour. Discard parsley and celery. Arrange rabbit on serving dish, thicken drippings with flour and pour gravy over the rabbit. Serves 4 to 6.

Scene on a Greek vase of about 500 B.C. shows fish seller cutting up tuna for a customer.

tuna

"The casting net is thrown down. The fishing net spread wide; and the tuna dart to and fro therein in the moonlight." Thus wrote the Greek historian, Herodotus who lived from 484 to 425 B.C.

Almost 500 years pass and the Kingdom of Heaven is likened to a net that is cast into the sea. (Matthew 13:47) Nineteen hundred years later men drop huge nets into the Pacific off the California coast and haul in their tuna. In this computerized world there is comfort in the thought that in some ways men's methods and lives have changed little.

45

Over 7,000 years ago the bones of a large tuna were left in the rubble of what later became ancient Troy. Modern searchers of ruins in the Near East have found other remains of tuna plus fish hooks nearly 4 inches long that must have been used for the big tunny of the Mediterranean. The Greeks were so fond of tuna they are said to have had "an almost cat-like love" for it. Their famous vase of Phylakopi, dated about 1500 B.C., shows men dancing with tuna in their hands. Many of their other works of art used tuna for decoration.

Unknown to the people of Bible days, along the coasts of South America other civilizations enjoyed this same fine fish. Before the time of Christ the people of Peru caught tuna from their remarkable reed boats. Inca emperors loved the fish so well they created a system of runners to bring tuna the same day it was caught from the coast 130 miles inland to the Inca capital of Cuzco.

Tuna to us, thunnos to the Greeks, tunny (rhymes with funny) to the people of the Mediterranean, xatunkamos to the Incas—all are names for a fish that has fed mankind for thousands of years and in the Twentieth Century is America's most popular seafood. Thus, across twin bridges of time and taste, this unchanging fish joins ancient civilizations to modern man.

In 1903 the first 17,000 *cans* of American tuna were packed in San Pedro, California. Today the U.S. produces about 18,000,000 *cases,* almost half the world output.

Tuna, like all fish, provides "complete" proteins, plus an impressive array of minerals and vitamins especially B_{12}. Ocean fish like tuna also contain iodine, essential to goiter prevention. These nutritional assets are capped with tuna's other values of polyunsaturated fats, ready digestibility and ease of preparation in a bewildering variety of recipes from salads to entrés.

You'll find tuna in a number of handy forms: solid pack perfect as the center of a salad platter or broken up for hot and cold dishes; chunk-style the favorite for use in casseroles, skillet dishes and salads; and grated or flake style, the shortcut to tuna mixtures with mayonnaise, sour cream or sandwich spreads. Incidentally, you can use white-meat and light-meat tuna interchangeably. For most recipes you needn't drain the oil from the tuna.

There are so many ways to prepare tuna it's impossible to pick out any *best* dishes. But here are some "goodies."

TUNA TIMBALES

1 can tuna (7 or 8 oz. size)
1 small onion, chopped
2 tbs. salad oil
3 eggs
1½ cups soft bread, cubed
2 tbs. lemon juice
1 tsp. minced parsley

Brown tuna and onion lightly in salad oil. Beat egg yolks and add bread, lemon juice and parsley. Combine with tuna. Beat egg whites until stiff and fold in. Turn into greased custard cups. Bake in pan of hot water at 350 degrees for 30 minutes or until firm. Serve with white sauce with 1 tsp. lemon juice and 1 tbs. chopped pimiento added. Makes 4 to 6 servings.

TUNA AND NOODLE CASSEROLE

1 can tuna, 7 oz. size
1 tbs. minced onion
1 tsp. Worcestershire sauce
1 can cream of mushroom soup, 10½ oz. size
  salt and pepper
2 cups cooked noodles
  potato chips
  butter or margarine

Break up the tuna in a bowl. Add the onion, Worcestershire sauce, mushroom soup and salt and pepper. Stir. Fold in the cooked noodles. Put it all in a buttered casserole, top with crumbled potato chips and dot with butter. Bake, uncovered, at 350° for about 30 minutes. Serves 4.

JELLIED TUNA-CUCUMBER SALAD

 1 tbs. gelatin
1½ cups water
 2 tbs. sugar
 ½ tsp. salt
 ¼ cup lemon juice
 1 tbs. grated onion
 1 cup cucumber, pared, seeded and diced
 1 can (7 or 8 oz. size) flaked tuna, drained

Soak gelatin in ½ cup cold water, then dissolve by adding 1 cup boiling water. Stir in sugar, salt, lemon juice and onion. Chill. When it starts to set add cucumber and tuna. Place in a wet mold. When firm unmold onto lettuce leaves. Garnish with mayonnaise. Serves 6.

fruits, melons

Hercules, the Greek God, in one of his adventures sought the "Golden apples" in the garden of the Hesperides. In this bas-relief from the Villa Albani, Rome he is shown seated in the garden below the tree of golden apples which many authorities believe was the name for apricots.

apples

Although the Bible does not mention the name of the fruit that Eve gave to Adam, tradition has perpetuated the belief it was an apple.

Elsewhere in the Bible, however, apples are mentioned several times by name. Solomon sings of them: "As the apple tree among the trees of the wood so is my beloved . . ." (Song of Solomon 2:3) "Comfort me with apples." (Song of Solomon 2:5) Despite these clear references some Biblical botanists believe these apples are actually apricots.

However, there are many signs that the apple of the Bible is indeed the apple we know or its forerunner, the crabapple. The fact is that apples are named in the records of *many* ancient people. Carbonized remains of them have been found in Neolithic Swiss lake dwellings. The Sumerians who flourished long before 2000 B.C. in Bible lands mention them in their texts. Their goddess Uttu is said to have been wooed by the great god Enki. But before she would submit to him she demanded he bring her gifts of "cucumbers, grapes and apples."

An Egyptian story that praised the city of Ramses around the end of the 13th century B.C. speaks of apples. The Hittites set such great store by them that their law code called for any man who destroyed an apple tree to pay six shekels of silver, a large sum in those days.

So it would appear the botanists may be wrong in denying the apple as a Biblical fruit. Certainly it was known to the people of later Old Testament times for the Greek Theophrastus, who was born in 370 B.C., writes of many kinds of apples and describes them in detail. The Roman gourmet Apicius gives two ways to preserve them. The first is to plunge the fruit for an instant into boiling water. His second method is to float them in honey so they do not touch each other.

The Greeks had a charming comparison of the apple with the setting sun. When the sky is green, yellow and red they said it is like an apple tree in bloom. Then as the sun is cut in two by the horizon it is like half an apple. When it sinks below the horizon and stars appear they are like the design of an apple when it is cut crosswise.

We feel there is no doubt the apple was well known and well loved by the ancients. The Hebrew word for apple is "tappuach." It appears as a proper name for various places and people in the Bible. "Tappuah on the border of Manasseh belonged to the children of Ephraim." (Joshua 17: 8) A descendant of Caleb bore the name. (I Chronicles 2: 43)

Although the apple is unquestionably of European origin the Americans have taken it as their own. The inspiring stories of Johnny Appleseed—who toured Ohio and Indiana in the last century preaching and planting apples—are evidence enough of the part apples played in our history. Today the U.S. produces more apples than any other country. There is no state in the Union that does not grow them. All told we harvest around 150 million bushels a year. A cultivated tree is in its prime at 50 years and may bear fruit until it is past 100.

APPLES IN ROBES

Pastry:
- 2 cups self-rising flour
- ¼ tsp. salt
- 4 tbs. sugar
- 1 cube margarine (½ cup)
- ¾ cup milk

Combine flour, salt and sugar and cut in margarine. Add milk and mix. Roll out on floured board and cut into squares large enough to wrap half an apple.

Filling:
- 4 apples, peeled, halved and cored
- ¼ cup sugar
- 1 tsp. cinnamon

Mix cinnamon and sugar. Put 1 tsp. in center of each pastry square. Place half an apple over it. Wrap carefully in pastry, sealing edges. Put in greased baking dish. Sprinkle remaining sugar over tops. Bake in 325 degree oven 30 minutes.

Sauce: Combine 1 cup sugar, 1 cup water, 1 tsp. vanilla, ½ tsp. cinnamon in pan and bring to boil. Pour over pastries after they have been in oven 20 minutes. Return to oven for 10 minutes more or until a fork pierces the apple filling easily. Serve hot with cream.

EDEN FALL SALAD

1 cup apple, diced
juice of ½ lemon
1 cup celery, diced
1 cup dark grapes, halved and seeded
½ cup walnut meats, broken
¾ cup mayonnaise
¼ cup cream
lettuce leaves

Choose firm, red apples. Core but do not peel. Cut in ½ inch cubes and sprinkle with lemon juice. Add celery, grapes and walnut meats. Mix mayonnaise and cream and blend into salad. Serve on crisp lettuce leaves. Makes 8 portions.

If you think of the apple as a crisp, fresh fruit and sometimes used in pies or sauce, you may find it difficult to believe that it can also play the part of a vegetable. The following casserole is a good example and a pleasant change. Try it in the company of your next pork roast.

APPLE CASSEROLE

4 tart apples, peeled, quartered and sliced
4 onions, same
6 slices of bacon, cut up and sautéed
¾ cup hot stock or water
½ tsp. salt
1 slice bread, crumbled
butter or margarine

In a buttered casserole arrange alternate layers of apples and onions sprinkling in the bacon bits as you go. Add the salt to the stock or water and pour over. Top with bread crumbs, dot with butter. Cover and bake at 350° for 30 minutes. Uncover and bake for another 15 minutes. Serves 4 to 6.

apricots

On the island of Cyprus at the eastern end of the Mediterranean apricots are still known as "golden apples." This is also the literal translation of their name in modern Greek.

As we trace the name farther into antiquity we become aware that in some cases the "apples" of the Bible should have been translated "apricots."

Some descriptions in the Bible fit the apricot more than the apple. "A word fitly spoken is like apples of gold in pictures of silver." (Proverbs 25:11) ". . . the smell of thy nose like apples;" (Song of Solomon 7:8) Certainly few fruits compare with the apricot in their delightful perfume and bright golden color among pale leaves.

Entirely aside from the question whether the Biblical "apples" should be translated "apricots" is the fact that apricots *did* grow in Bible lands well before the time of Jesus. Clay tablets from the Tigris-Euphrates delta at the head of the Persian Gulf have references to apricots. They are dated around 2000 B.C. Alexander the Great (356 to 323 B.C.) was one of the great conquerors of all time. After his victories in Asia Minor he is said to have brought the apricot to Greece. Pliny and Columella, Latin writers in the first century A.D., knew the fruit well.

In Greek mythology apricots as "golden apples" played many parts. At a marriage ceremony among the gods, Eris, god of Discord, was conspicuous by his absence for he had not been invited. Entering, nonetheless, he threw on the banquet table "a golden apple for the most beautiful woman present." Immediately three vain goddesses, Juno, Minerva and Venus claimed the apricot. Venus won the judgment and brought down the wrath of the other two ladies upon poor Paris, who was the judge in the case.

If the gods of ancient Greece ever ate apricots as they flew through the skies they have their counterparts today in our Gemini V astronauts. Because apricot pudding was on the carefully chosen menu for this eight day flight.

Among popular fruits apricots are far and away the richest in vitamin A. Three fresh ones contain about 2,890 International Units of vitamin A. When canned they have just slightly less; but when dried a cupful contains 16,390 units. Just one-third cup of dried apricots will supply the vitamin A needs of the average child and practically all those for an adult.

With fresh 'cots on the market in the summer months we scarcely need point out the deliciousness of this beautiful and luscious fruit. However, far more apricots are consumed in canned or dried form so here are recipes for these two most popular forms of apricots.

KING SOLOMON'S GOLD
- 8 oz. package dried apricots
- 3 cups water
- 1½ tbs. gelatin
- 1½ cups sugar
- 3 tbs. lemon juice
- 4 egg whites
- ⅛ tsp. salt

Add 2 cups water to the apricots in a sauce pan and place over low heat. Bring to boil and simmer until the juice is absorbed and the fruit is very tender—about 30 minutes. Cool. Mix sugar with ½ cup water and heat until dissolved. Soak gelatine in ½ cup water and dissolve in sugar mixture. Add lemon juice and let cool. Whirl the apricots and half the sugar mixture in a blender or beat until smooth. Add remaining syrup and mix well. Beat egg whites and salt until stiff and fold in. Place in wet mold and chill until set. Serve with whipped cream. Enough for 8.

APRICOTS ABIGAIL (a fritter)
- 1 large can apricots, halves, drained
- 2 eggs
- ⅔ cup milk or water
- 1 tbs. lemon juice
- 1 tbs. melted butter
- 1 cup flour, sifted
- 2 tbs. sugar
- ¼ tsp. salt

Beat egg yolks and add milk or water, lemon juice and butter. Resift flour with salt and sugar and add to yolks, stirring well. Beat egg whites with a dash of salt until stiff. Then fold into the batter. Dip apricots in the batter and sauté in butter until delicately browned, turning just once. Drain on paper towels and serve hot. May be sprinkled with powdered sugar or served with butter and syrup.

A perfect accompaniment to roast duck or goose is the tart-sweet combination that follows. Also excellent with ham or pork roasts.

GLAZED APRICOTS

Put dried apricots and prunes in a colander over boiling water. Steam 25 to 30 minutes, until almost tender. Remove pits. Place fruits alternately on skewers. Brush them with melted butter. Roll them in brown sugar. Bake for the last 15 to 20 minutes with the roast. When ready to serve, sprinkle again with brown sugar. Place under broiler to glaze. Watch closely. The sugar burns easily.

Spicy apricots can be served either hot or cold. They go very well with ham or roasted beef.

SPICY APRICOTS

1 1 lb. 13 oz. can whole apricots
2 tbs. brown sugar
¼ tsp. ginger
½ tsp. cinnamon
1 tbs. vinegar

Mix the seasonings together in a little of the juice. Put all ingredients in a saucepan. Bring to a boil, then reduce heat. Let simmer for 15 minutes.

CAROB

Carob pods hanging among leaves. The tree is an evergreen with brown pods that vary in length from 4 to 12 inches. Inside are flinty, dark brown seeds about the size and shape of watermelon seeds.

Precious jewels and carob beans have been cherished by mankind for thousands of years. Perhaps it is not strange then that the word "carat" which is used to measure the weight of gem stones is derived from the Arabic word "qirat" which in turn comes from the Greek "keration" meaning carob bean or small weight.

At the other end of the spectrum we find the Bible telling us of the prodigal son who "would fain have filled his belly with the husks that the swine did eat. . . ." (Luke 15:16) Those husks were carob pods that had fallen beneath the tree and were relished by men and animals alike. Many Bible scholars are convinced that the "locusts" John the Baptist ate were carob beans. This is why the carob is still known popularly as St. John's bread and sometimes as locust pod. (Matthew 3:4)

In the Talmud the carob is often mentioned. One delightful story from this ancient Jewish source book tells of a young rabbi who came upon an old man planting a carob seed beside the road. When the rabbi remarked that the man would be long dead when the tree bore fruit the old man replied: "I plant not for myself but for those who come after me." Then, shades of Rip van Winkle, the young rabbi lay down to rest. Seventy years later he awoke to find the carob tree full of fruit and himself an old man in unfamiliar surroundings.

Theophrastus the fourth century B.C. Greek was very familiar with the carob. He remarked that some people in his day called it the Egyptian fig. Certainly the Egyptians knew it. From a temple at Edfu comes an ancient prescription whose ingredients include essence of carob bean.

If you think we Americans do not use carob you'll be surprised that we import about 17,000,000 pounds each year from Mediterranean countries. The carob is used in flour form for cooking, in a delectable candy bar and as a dietetic substitute for chocolate. By-products go into everything from ice cream to mustard.

The flavor of carob has been described as a honey-date-chocolate combination. Certainly it is sweet for it is almost 50% sugar. When roasted and ground it gives a deep chocolate color to food and in flavor is like milk chocolate. The easily digested carob is so full of trace minerals that its full nutritional value has not been probed. However, we do know it contains calcium, potassium, magnesium, phosphorus plus small amounts of vitamins A, B_1, B_2 and a relatively large amount of niacin.

The flour is used medicinally to treat diarrhea. Such physiological values come from the high content of pectin, lignin and hemicellulose. But the biggest use of carob is for food. It is especially recommended for people allergic to chocolate. However, its delicate chocolate flavor has contributed more than anything else to its popularity. Its uses range widely from bread (to which carob flour gives color and flavor) to beverages, candy, icings and other confections.

A sweet chocolate-like syrup to serve over ice cream or mix with milk may be made in minutes with carob powder.

CAROB SYRUP

1 cup sugar
½ cup water
¼ cup carob

Mix and bring to a boil. Cook for 3 minutes. Cool and refrigerate. Will keep for weeks.

For a slightly heavier syrup and one with a sharper, but pleasant change-of-pace-taste try substituting ½ cup light honey for ½ cup of the sugar in the recipe above.

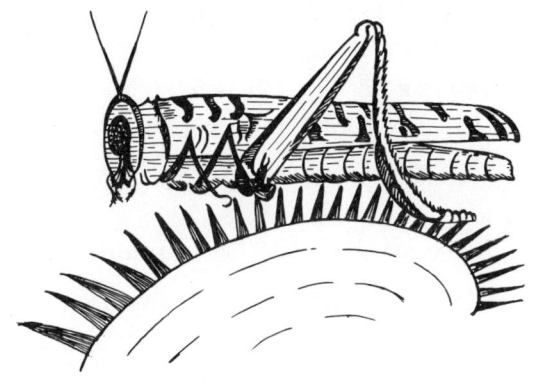

"... and his meat was locusts and wild honey." (Matthew 3:4 King James) This was the food of John the Baptist in the wilderness. There is a debate whether the "locusts" were indeed the locust shown here from a tomb painting of Haremhab, 15th century B.C. Pharaoh. Some Bible scholars believe the reference is to carob pods which are also called "locust pods" based on this belief.

Try this recipe on your family without telling them the ingredients and see if they don't love your new "chocolate" spice cake.

ST. JOHN'S CAKE

2 cups sugar
½ cup butter or margarine
4 eggs
6 tbs. carob powder
2 cups flour, sifted before measuring
1 tsp. cinnamon
¼ tsp. cloves
2 tsp. baking powder
¼ tsp. salt
1 cup milk

Beat butter until soft and cream sugar in until light. Separate eggs and beat yolks in one at a time. Stir carob powder into ¼ cup of water and add. Re-sift flour with cinnamon, cloves, baking powder and salt. Add to the batter alternately with milk. Whip egg whites with an extra dash of salt until stiff and fold lightly into cake mixture. Bake in three greased 9 inch layer pans at 375 degrees for about 30 minutes. Cool and spread with carob icing.

CAROB ICING (uncooked)

4 tbs. butter or margarine
1½ cups powdered milk
1 cup carob powder
½ cup honey
6 tbs. cream
1 tsp. vanilla

Cream butter and powdered milk with beater until texture is like corn meal. Add honey and vanilla. Beat well. Add carob powder beating at lowest speed until blended. Add cream a tablespoonful at a time, beating well.

dates

Woven into the center of the tapestry of the history of man in the brightest color is the date palm.

For the Sumerians of the Tigris-Euphrates valley, who created a high civilization as much as 7,000 years ago, the date was their fruit par excellence. It flourished in huge groves where the trees had their "feet in water and their head in the fires of heaven." Sumerian clay tablets dated 4,000 years ago mention dates often as "provisions for the king's house," or as offerings to their gods. Sumerian texts list nearly 150 words for the various kinds of palms and their parts.

When the children of Israel departed from the city of Rameses in Egypt (Exodus 12:37) they left behind them a beautiful, fruitful metropolis which Egyptian texts tell us grew luscious dates "by its river banks." King Solomon's temple was decorated with carvings of the date palm (I Kings 6:29 & 32). His city of Tadmor (now the oasis of Palmyra) means "city of palms." The name Bethany is translated "house of dates." A Jewish symbol of grace and elegance was the date palm which they called tamar. So highly did they regard it that they named women Tamar or Tamarah. There are nine Bible references to women of this name.

Jericho is referred to in II Chronicles 28:15 as the city of palm trees. It is sad that today in the Holy Land the date palm is almost a thing of the past. Yet there is evidence that at one time the whole Jordan valley from the shores of Gennesaret (Sea of Galilee) to the end of the Dead Sea was covered with date palms. Today all that is left are petrified date palm trunks piled at the end of the Dead Sea and fossilized palm fronds near the ancient city of Engedi which II Chronicles 20:2 tells us was known also as Hazezon-tamar "felling of the palm trees."

Sumerian sources and clay tablets dated 2500 B.C. mention superb dates from "Dilmun." This is the island of Bahrein off the coast of Arabia in the Persian Gulf opposite Hasa. To this day the Khalasa date of Hasa is considered the world's finest. A few Khalasas now grow in Arizona and the Coachella valley of California.

Although the U.S. continues to import dates from the lands of their origin we now produce a good crop in the Coachella valley. Most popular is the Deglet Noor "date of light." It varies from light gold to deep mahogany in color and makes magnificent eating.

The date is particularly associated with Easter time for its palm branches are still carried by millions of Christians on Palm Sunday. This recalls the entry of Jesus into

Jerusalem as told in John 12:12 & 13; ". . . when they heard that Jesus was coming to Jerusalem, took branches of palm trees, and went forth to meet him. . . ." For the Jews the date palm symbolizes the harvest season. It is still carried at their ceremonies during the Feast of Tabernacles, Sukkot.

TAMARAH PIE

    1 cup dates, pitted and cut up
    1 cup water
    ⅓ cup sugar
    3 tbs. cornstarch
    ¼ tsp. salt
    1 cup nutmeats of your choice, chopped
    ¼ cup orange juice
    1 tbs. orange rind, grated

Boil dates in the water for 3 minutes. Mix sugar, cornstarch, salt together. Stir into dates. Boil one minute stirring constantly. Remove from heat. Add nutmeats, orange rind and juice. Pour into an unbaked pie shell. Place strips of pastry dough in a lattice pattern on top. Bake at 400 degrees for 30 minutes. Cut in thin slices. Serve with sour cream or whipped cream. Makes a fairly thin pie but quite rich. Sweetness may be increased by using less orange rind.

DATE CAKE

3 eggs
¼ tsp. salt
½ tsp. vanilla
1 cup sugar
⅓ cup flour
1 tsp. baking powder
1 cup walnuts, coarsely chopped
1 cup dates, coarsely cut up

Separate the eggs. Add the salt to the whites and beat until very stiff. Set aside. Beat the yolks until creamy, stir in sugar and vanilla. Sift flour and baking powder together and add to yolks. Stir in nuts and dates then fold in egg whites. Pour into buttered 8"x8" cake pan and bake at 300° for 45 minutes.

TADMOR DELIGHT

2 cups sugar
1 cup milk
¼ cup butter or margarine
½ pound dates, cut up
1 cup nutmeats of your choice

Boil the sugar, milk and butter until it reaches 235 degrees or forms a soft ball in cold water. Add dates. Continue to cook over low heat stirring constantly until it becomes very thick and starts to follow spoon as you stir. Remove from heat and add nutmeats. Beat with spoon until it starts to set. Then pour in buttered pan to cool.

figs

The first fruit to be mentioned specifically in the Bible is the fig: Adam and Eve "sewed fig leaves together and made themselves aprons." Gen. 3:7 (King James)

When Abigail sought to make peace with David one of the gifts she offered was figs. (I Sam. 25:18) Isaiah prescribed figs to heal King Hezekiah's boils. (II Kings 20:7) Even now some Swiss doctors use finely chopped figs steamed in milk for certain kinds of abscesses.

Mummy cases made from the wood of the sycamore fig have been found in Egyptian tombs over 3,000 years old. In the Near East this wood still is used to make furniture; and fig leaves are sewed together to make baskets, dishes and umbrellas. The shade of a fig tree is considered in the Near East to be fresher and cooler than a tent. With all its uses it is small wonder the fig was so highly regarded in Bible days. To sit under your own vine and fig tree became the sign of peace and plenty. (Micah 4:4)

The major fig crop in the U.S. is produced in California with minor contributions from southern states like Texas, S. Carolina, Florida and other south Atlantic states. There are four principal commercial varieties. The Black Mission was brought to California by the padres who founded the Missions. It is not so large as some varieties but its high sugar content and rather small seeds make it excellent eating.

The best known white figs are "white Adriatic," "kadota" and "Calimyrna." The latter is the name for California figs that have been developed from an imported variety named after the ancient town of Smyrna (now Izmir) on the Aegean Sea in Turkey. Calimyrna figs, often used in gift packs, are large with a rich yellow color, full of edible seeds that give them a pleasing nut-like flavor.

Figs are a natural confection whether you eat them fresh, canned or dried. They have a delectable, full flavor because they are permitted to ripen on the tree before they are picked. Dried figs are a superb source of quick energy for active children or adults since they contain over 55% natural fruit sugar plus large amounts of iron, vitamin B_1 and calcium.

Try the "Festive Figs" described below as a sweet repetition of the gift figs offered to David by those who came to make him king. The story is told in I Chronicles 12:40.

FESTIVE FIGS

Use dried whole figs. In one side make full length slit. Stuff with any of the following goodies: salted almonds, cashews or Brazil nuts, wedge of candied ginger, half of mint or wintergreen cream patties, an after-dinner mint, chopped salted peanuts with peanut butter, shredded coconut with cashew nut, fresh kumquat halves or fresh cranberries. Or, invent your own stuffing. It's fun!

You might try "sherried figs" too. Place 12 or more figs in a bowl. Cover with dry sherry wine. Let stand for 24 hours or more. Turn occasionally so all figs get well soaked. Drain. Roll lightly in confectioner's sugar. Use remaining sherry for pudding sauce.

BAKED CHRISTMAS PUDDING

¼ cup butter or margarine
½ cup molasses
1 egg
1 cup figs, chopped
½ cup walnut meats, chopped
1 tsp. lemon rind, grated
¼ tsp. baking soda
½ cup sour milk
1¼ cups flour, sifted before measuring
1 tsp. baking powder
½ tsp. cinnamon
½ tsp. salt
¼ tsp. nutmeg

Beat butter until soft. Add molasses and eggs and beat well. Stir in figs, nut meats and lemon rind. Put soda into sour milk, stir and add. Re-sift flour with remaining dry ingredients and stir into batter. Bake in greased loaf pan at 325 degrees for 50 minutes. Serves 8.

Serve hot with the following:

SAUCE

2 eggs
½ cup powdered sugar
2 tbs. brandy
(or sherry wine or 1½ tsp. vanilla)
1 cup whipping cream

Separate eggs. Beat yolks and stir in powdered sugar and brandy. Whip cream until stiff. In separate bowl beat egg whites until stiff. Fold the cream into the yolk mixture. Then fold in egg whites.

Men who trekked across great deserts with camel caravans carried their food with them. Modern hikers and back packers have borrowed a secret from these ancients. A combination of dried fruits and nuts, ground together, makes a tasty and highly nutritious meal. It requires no cooking, takes little space in a pack, weighs only a fraction of equivalent foods and keeps well.

Try the recipe below or substitute your favorite dried fruits and nuts. If you use fruits your children like, you can offer them a nutritious fruit bar when they ask for candy.

CARAVAN CANDY

½ cup (about 15) small figs, stemmed
½ cup (about 20) dates, pitted
1 cup walnut meats
rind of 1 orange, grated
2 tbs. orange juice
powdered sugar

Put fruit and nuts through the food chopper, alternating to help mix them. Add the orange rind and juice. Knead with fingers to mix well. Pull off about 1 tbs. at a time, roll into a ball, flatten and roll in powdered sugar. If you are packing the bars, it helps to separate them by wrapping in small pieces of waxed paper.

GRAPES

Slaves pick grapes in this painting from the 15th century B.C. in the tomb of Nakht. Thebes, Egypt.

Dig where you will in the remains of the ancient Near East—on the island of Crete, in the ruins of Lachish near the Gaza strip, among the tombs of Egyptian Pharaohs or the Babylonian plains—and you are likely to find seeds, drawings or written records of one of mankind's oldest fruits, the grape. To this very day there are more grapes grown than any other fruit.

Grapes are the first plant the Bible mentions as being under cultivation. After the flood "... Noah began to be a husbandman, and he planted a vineyard...." (Genesis 9:20) From this point on the Bible abounds with references to grapes and their products. It was forbidden to glean a vineyard so some grapes would be left for the poor and the stranger who passed by. (Leviticus 19:10; Deut. 24:21) Jesus called himself "the true vine." (John 15:1)

In Numbers 13:17 to 25 is told the story of Moses' vanguard sent to look over the land of Canaan. They "came unto Hebron" which is still a city in present day Israel just 28 miles south of Jerusalem. At the brook Eshcol (literal meaning "grapes") they cut down a bunch of grapes so large they had to carry it between them on a staff.

During the 215 years of Hebrew captivity in Egypt the Jews became quite familiar with grapes and their cultivation because the Egyptians grew grapes over 6,000 years ago. Their contemporaries, the Sumerians in the Tigris-Euphrates valley, have left records of a number of varieties: white, fox-grapes, Elamite, sweet grapes, etc.

For the people of Bible days the grape vine yielded fresh fruit and raisins, grape leaves for cooking, wine, vinegar, fresh juice called "must" and a sweet syrup, "dibs" made by boiling down the fresh juice until it is about the consistency of molasses. No wonder that everywhere in the Bible the grape vine is used as a symbol of peace and plenty, of the good life.

Our much loved white Thompson seedless is originally from the Old World. Now, forty-eight percent of California's half million acres of vineyards are planted to this variety. They come on the market about mid-July and remain available until almost Christmas. Other popular varieties like Emperor and Tokay are a fall fruit.

The ancient Persians believed that dried red grapes eaten before breakfast would improve the memory. But dry, fresh or cooked, grapes are a delectable food. If you haven't cooked with them here are recipes guaranteed to convince you grapes should be on your menus.

A combination of fresh fruits tastefully arranged in a low bowl makes a beautiful centerpiece for a summer or early fall dinner. Your guests can serve themselves with their choice of these fruits for dessert, thus, it can serve two purposes. A variety of grapes, large and small, of different colors, add a great deal to the beauty of a fruit bowl. Here is a way to increase the interest and natural beauty.

FROST-ON-THE-GRAPES

Wash bunches of grapes under running water and set aside to dry on paper towels. Beat an egg white until frothy, then lightly brush over the grapes. Sprinkle with sugar. Let dry thoroughly before arranging in the bowl.

SOLE VERONIQUE

- 12 small filets of sole
- 1 tsp. salt
- 1½ cups water
- 1 chicken bouillon cube
- 2 bay leaves
- 6 whole peppercorns
- 4 slices lemon
- 1 sprig parsley
- 1 cup white grapes halved and seeded (or seedless grapes, halved)
- 3 tbs. butter or margarine
- 1 tbs. flour
- ½ cup cream

Salt filets. Roll up from small end and secure with toothpick. Dissolve bouillon cube in water in heavy pan and arrange rolled fillets in it. Add bay leaves, peppercorns, lemon slices, parsley. Cover and cook over low heat 12 minutes. Discard bay leaves, peppercorns, lemon and parsley. Carefully remove filets to heated platter. Pour grapes over them and keep hot. Meanwhile, reduce liquid in pan to ½ cup. Stir in creamed butter and flour, blending and cooking until smooth. Add cream and cook until slightly thickened. Pour sauce over filets. Put under broiler for a minute or two until a dull glaze appears on grapes. Be careful not to brown. Serves six.

VINE 'N SEA SALAD

  2 cups cooked shrimp (about 1 lb.)
  1 cup Thompson seedless grapes, halved (or other white grapes seeded and halved)
  1 cup diced celery
  1 tsp. salt
  ¼ tsp. pepper
  2 tsp. lemon juice
  ½ cup mayonnaise
    crisp lettuce leaves

Combine shrimp, grapes, celery, salt and pepper. Mix lemon juice into mayonnaise and blend. Pour over salad and toss lightly. Chill. Serve on crisp lettuce leaves. Makes four generous servings for a light, cool but filling luncheon when served with hot bread and a beverage.

ESHCOL SURPRISE

  fresh pears, halved and cored
  small seedless grapes
  cream cheese
  cream
  leaves for garnish

Wash and halve the pears, remove core, stem and bud. Place each, cut side down on a salad plate. Add a little cream to the cream cheese and work it in so that it can be spread over the pear about ¼ inch thick. Starting at the stem end gently press the grapes into the cheese spread to make it look like a bunch of grapes. Garnish at the top with small grape or ivy leaves.

muskmelons

When the Israelites wandered in the wilderness they recalled, among other foods, the melons they had when they were slaves in Egypt. (See Numbers 11:5) This scene shows slaves at work in an Egyptian brickyard. Tomb painting 15th century B.C.

All cantaloupes are muskmelons but not all muskmelons are cantaloupes. Cantaloupes are the first muskmelons to appear in the summer. Other members of the family like Casaba, Honey Dew, Honey Ball and Persian, are the so-called winter melons on the market a little later.

When the Israelites wandered in the wilderness after their departure from Egypt they longed for the melons they had enjoyed in the land of the Pharaohs. (Numbers 11:5) Biblical botanists are convinced they spoke of muskmelons and watermelons since both have been cultivated for thousands of years in Egypt. Ancient Egyptian texts speak of "melons growing on the sands," and funerary paintings from that same land show pictures of muskmelons as far back as 2400 B.C. Sumerian records from 2000 B.C. and before mention melons.

Pliny, the Latin writer of the first century A.D. aptly described a characteristic of muskmelons that is true of no other garden crop i.e. the fact that when ripe they part spontaneously from their stem. In his day they were served often with a dressing made of pepper, herbs, honey and vinegar.

It is generally agreed among botanists that the muskmelon originated in the ancient lands of the Medes and Persians. In fact, the word "musk" is Persian for a kind of perfume. Oddly the name "cantaloupe" comes from an area, Cantalupo in Italy, where the true cantaloupe was introduced from Armenia. It is a hardshelled or rock melon that is little grown outside the Mediterranean lands. Our cantaloupe has a soft rind and is considerably different from the botanically true cantaloupe.

Like so many of our fruits and vegetables the muskmelon was brought to America by Columbus on his second voyage. But it was not until after the Civil War that they became a popular market crop.

As might be expected most muskmelons have about the same nutrients. But there is one important exception. The cantaloupe has a great deal more Vitamin A in its orange-colored flesh—almost 100 times more, for instance —than Casabas or Honey Dews.

When you're buying a muskmelon these are the things to look for: a ripe cantaloupe has a definite fragrance at the stem end, the netting is well raised, coarse, dry and grayish in color with the background behind the netting light in color. Ripe Casabas, which are plentiful during October and November, have a rough rind and wrinkled furrows lengthwise with no netting and a buttery-yellow rind. They have little fragrance compared with other melons. Persian melons have a deep green rind evenly covered with a fine netting similar to a cantaloupe with a rich orange-pink flesh and pleasant aroma.

Usually melons are eaten "as is" so most recipes cover various ways to serve them fresh. Here are some suggestions that will add variety to your melon dishes plus one recipe for a very unusual pie. No one will ever guess its delicate flavor source.

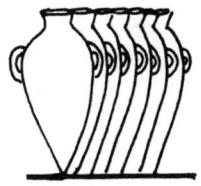

MIRIAM'S MELON CUP

Use Honey Dew, watermelon, cantaloupe or other melons cut into balls. A combination of several colors is best. For each cup of melon balls use 1 tbs. honey dissolved in 1 tbs. lemon juice as a dressing. Toss lightly and serve in chilled sherbet glasses. Garnish with a sprig of fresh mint.

This recipe is similar to one served in Rome at the time of Christ. But the pie that follows is an original that, as we said above, has a delicate flavor no one will ever be able to "guess."

PERSIAN PIE

Crust:

    1½ cups graham cracker crumbs
    ½ cup powdered sugar
    6 tbs. melted butter
    dash of salt

Mix well and press into bottom and sides of pie pan. Bake at 350° for 10 to 12 minutes. Cool.

Filling:

    2 cups melon, whirled in blender before measuring
    1 tbs. gelatin
    ¼ cup lemon juice
    4 eggs
    ¾ cup sugar
    ½ tsp. salt
    ¼ cup water

Pare the melon and remove seeds, dice and blend at top speed. Add melon until you have 2 cups (a small melon should do it). Melt gelatin in lemon juice and set aside. Beat egg yolks in top of double boiler, add ¼ cup sugar, salt and water. Cook over boiling water to a custard like consistency. Add gelatin and stir well. Set aside to cool. Beat the egg whites until stiff and add remaining ½ cup sugar slowly while still beating. Fold together the custard, egg whites and melon. Fill the pie shell heaping full and refrigerate. Serve with a small sprig of mint on each piece of pie.

    In ICED TEA add a few melon balls or cubes just before serving to create a fresh taste. As a GARNISH for melon cups place a few melon balls or cubes in each of several small glasses. Cover with cold water and add food colorings. Most appetizing colors are red, green, yellow and orange. Let stand in refrigerator for several hours or overnight if you want deep shades.

olives

Today on the outskirts of Jerusalem in the garden of Gethsemane stand eight gnarled olive trees. They are hundreds of years old and it is believed that their seeds came from the very trees that witnessed the agony of Christ when he was betrayed and ultimately crucified.

From Genesis to Revelation the olive wends its way through the Bible as a symbol of peace and friendship. The first mention is Genesis 8:11 in the story of Noah and the Ark. For the second time he had sent forth a dove. "And the dove came in to him in the evening, and, lo, in her mouth was an olive leaf plucked off; so Noah knew that the waters were abated from off the earth." This was the first sign that God's wrath had been satisfied. From that time forward an olive branch has been a token of tranquillity and forgiveness, of love and divine blessing.

The fruit and its oil made it the most important and most loved tree of the scriptures. Practically every village in ancient Palestine had its olive grove. To this very day olive trees abound in the Holy Land from the vale of Shechem to Esdraelon, all over the lower slopes of the valleys around Hebron to the plains of Gilead.

In Judges 9:8 and 9 is told the delightful story of all the trees who sought a leader. The first to whom they turned was the olive tree. Though it declined the honor it became the very symbol of Israel. When Jesus taught by day he retired at night to the Mount of Olives.

Among medieval Christians and some today there lives a legend about the olive that illustrates the sanctity surrounding it. "As Adam lay on his death bed the Angel guarding the Garden of Eden gave Seth three seeds: olive, cypress and cedar. When planted they formed a single tree with three trunks, one for each of the seeds. Under this tree David wept as he contemplated his sins. When Solomon cut down the tree he found it could not be hewn. So it was thrown into a marsh where it formed a bridge for the Queen of Sheba. In the end its wood was made into the cross on which Jesus was crucified."

Olives are eaten so extensively in the Near East they have become a necessity at practically every meal from breakfast to supper. They are, of course, eaten both ripe and green. If you've ever been tempted by a ripe olive shining in the sun on the tree you may have discovered that it is a very bitter fruit to the taste when fresh. The secret of pickling to make it edible has been known for thousands of years. In the United States, California produces practically 99% of all American grown olives.

There are four principal varieties: Mission, the first ones planted by the early Padres; Manzanillo from Spain, meaning "little apple;" Sevillano, which comes from around Seville, Spain; and Ascolano which is originally from Italy. Harvesting is from September to February.

SALAD OF SHEBA

1 16 oz. can ripe pitted olives, halved
2 large fresh tomatoes, peeled and diced
1 cucumber, peeled and diced
1 green pepper, cut up
½ cup onion, chopped
½ cup parsley, minced
3 tbs. lemon juice
2 tbs. olive oil
1 tsp. salt
¼ tsp. basil
⅛ tsp. pepper
⅛ tsp. garlic powder

Put olives, tomatoes, cucumber, pepper and onion in a bowl. Sprinkle parsley over. Put remaining ingredients in a covered jar. Shake the dressing well. Pour over salad and toss lightly to mix. Chill for several hours. Serve in lettuce cups. Serves 6.

OLIVE SAUCE ITALIANO

2 tbs. butter
1 slice onion
2 tbs. flour
1 cup broth, stock or consommé
12 stuffed green olives, sliced

Melt butter in a saucepan and sauté onion until light brown. Remove onion. Stir in flour. Cook and stir until browned. Stir in liquid slowly. Continue to stir and cook until smooth. Add sliced olives. Pour on left-over roast or other meat dishes. Makes 1 cup sauce.

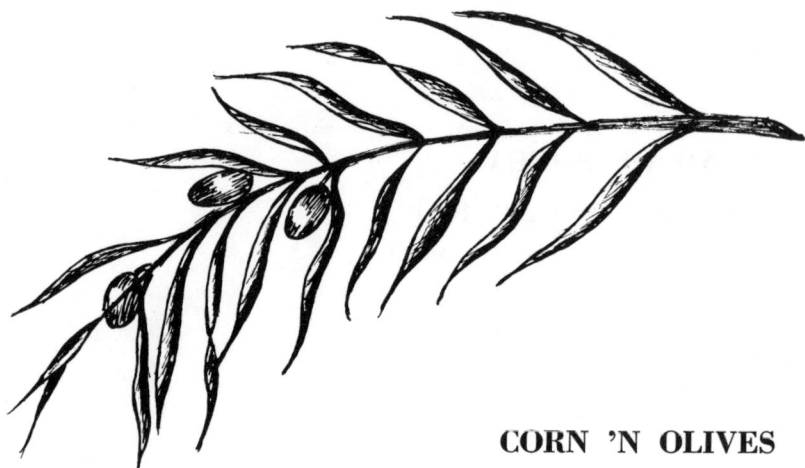

CORN 'N OLIVES

Filling:

- 1 lb. lean ground beef
- 1 cup ripe olives, pitted and sliced
- 1 cup onion, chopped
- 1 large green pepper, chopped
- 1 large rib celery, chopped
- 2 cups tomatoes, peeled and cut up
- 1 cup cooked corn (8 or 9 oz. can)
- 2 cloves garlic, crushed
- 1 tbs. chili powder
- 2 tsp. salt
- 1 cup grated cheese

Brown meat in heavy skillet. Add remaining ingredients—except cheese—and let simmer about 20 minutes while you make the crust.

Crust:

- 2½ cups yellow corn meal
- 2 tsp. salt
- 1 tsp. chili powder
- 5 cups cold water

Combine all ingredients in a saucepan. Cook over medium heat, stirring until thickened—about 15 minutes. Line sides and bottom of a buttered, 2 quart rectangular casserole with about ⅔ of the mixture. Add filling (see above) and cover top with small spoonfuls of the crust. Sprinkle with the grated cheese. Bake at 350 degrees about 45 minutes. Serves 8 to 10.

pomegranates

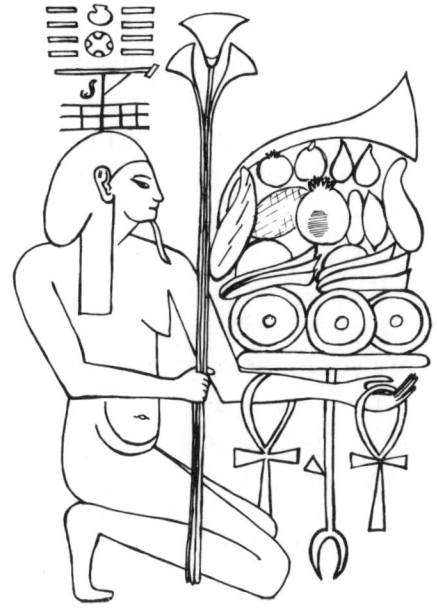

An offering to the gods is shown in this carved relief from ancient Egypt. Note the pomegranate in the center of the pile of fruit.

"Your cheeks are like halves of a pomegranate," sang Solomon to his beloved. (Song of Solomon 4:3 RSV) Upon the hem of the garment of the high priest the Lord commanded should be embroidered "a golden bell and a pomegranate, a golden bell and a pomegranate." (Exodus 28:34)

"Saul tarried under a pomegranate tree." (I Samuel 14:2) Moses told of the promised land where grew "vines and fig trees, and pomegranates." (Deut. 8:8) The temple of Solomon was generously decorated with pomegranates. (I Kings 7:18 & 20)

There's little doubt the people of Bible days loved this remarkable fruit. In fact, an ancient legend claims that the "tree of life" in the garden of Eden was the pomegranate. In Egypt it was a sacred fruit that appears clearly and frequently in their art and sculpture. Even the flowers were so well loved that they were used as the design for Solomon's crown which remained for centuries as the classic form of all crowns. On this score a Greek myth tells of a beautiful nymph who had been informed by an oracle she would some day wear a crown. Sure enough, when Bacchus transformed her into a pomegranate tree he gave her blooms shaped like crowns.

The tree itself as well as flowers and fruit is quite beautiful. Its longevity is legendary. Specimens over 200 years old have been known to bear fruit. Uses of the pomegranate are many. The Moors introduced to Spain a method of tanning leather with pomegranates that made Cordova famous for its leatherwork. It is very likely the first sherbet was pomegranate juice mixed with snow. Certainly it was well known in Bible times as a cooling drink as well as the basis for spiced wine. The seeds were dried and sprinkled on foods for flavor or eaten as a condiment. In Iran, the land of the Persians, they make thick soups and stews with pomegranates, meat and vegetables.

Colors of different species run from yellow with a blush of red to the deep red and even purple of the pomegranates usually found on the American market. The skin is thick and filled with literally hundreds of seeds. No wonder it was regarded as a fertility symbol. The flavor of the red, juicy pulp is slightly acid and unique.

Pomegranates are on the market from September to December. If you haven't tried them you'll be surprised to find how many ways they can be served. First of all they can be eaten fresh. Just break one open and spoon out the juicy seeds. Some people spit out the seeds. Others chew them up just as they do grape seeds.

For a garnish on fruit salad or dessert sprinkle some of the seeds over the top. If you'd like to add a tangy new flavor to your iced tea, squeeze a bit of fresh pomegranate juice into it. Lemonade turns pink and delicious with pomegranate juice. To squeeze, work the seedy pulp through a colander or twist in a heavy cheesecloth.

As an appetizer mix fresh pomegranate seeds with filberts or walnuts. Stir in a bit of honey and serve in tiny bowls for the stunning first course of an intimate dinner. Make the servings small. After dinner a little cup of pomegranate seeds makes an unusual and delectable combination with Camembert cheese and crackers.

Pomegranate juice is the basis of true Grenadine syrup. This sweetened juice has a multitude of uses. Of course, the children's cocktail that used to be known as a "Shirley Temple" and later as a "Batman" is made with Grenadine and ginger ale. But try it as a flavoring in other ways. For instance, add a bit to your pancake syrup for something different at your next breakfast. It's easy to use in gelatin desserts, cake icing, fruit drinks and pudding sauces.

For fruit salad dressing stir 4 tbs. Grenadine into a half cup of French dressing. As a topping for melons or melon compote beat 8 oz. of honey for about 6 minutes. Add 2 tbs. Grenadine and a pinch of salt. Continue beating 2 more minutes.

Lastly use the whole fruit as part of your centerpiece whether it's made of flowers or fruit. If you can get hold of some of the leafy branches you'll have an arrangement reminiscent of Old Testament times.

Strange though it may seem to us today, insects were eaten freely in Bible days. (See Leviticus 11:22) In this scene, the first servant carries locusts for a banquet at the palace of Asurbanipal at Nineveh in Assyria. Second servant brings pomegranates.

If you dare to be different you can tell your friends what goes into this soup. Or you can simply serve it and let them enjoy its remarkable flavor before you tell them. Even more fun, let them try to guess. Any way you decide to proceed, we think you'll enjoy this dish which had its beginning in ancient Persia.

SULTAN'S SOUP

2 cups pomegranate juice
   (an acceptable substitute
   if pomegranates are
   not available is:
   1½ cups cranberry juice
   ½ cup orange juice)
1 lb. lean ground meat (lamb, beef or veal)
1 tsp. salt
½ tsp. pepper
½ tsp. cloves
½ tsp. turmeric
4 tbs. olive oil
1 cup parsley, minced
1 tbs. mint, minced
1 onion, minced
1 10½ oz. can beef consommé

Sprinkle the salt, pepper, cloves and turmeric over the meat and work it in with your fingers. Shape into very small (marble size) meat balls rolling them in your palms to make them firm.

Put olive oil in a heavy saucepan, add parsley, mint and onion and sauté lightly. Add meat balls and brown well, stirring gently from time to time. Add consommé and pomegranate juice; cover and simmer for half an hour.

With Bedouin Bread and a salad will serve 4. As a first course for dinner, 8.

Raisins were used to pay taxes to King David about 1000 B.C. by the Israelites.

RAISINS

Raisins are undoubtedly as ancient a food as grapes, for a few hot days under a clear sun will turn grapes into raisins right on the vine. Seeds of grapes have been found in the oldest tombs of Egypt.

In stories about David told in first and second Samuel and in first Chronicles raisins are frequently mentioned. Abigail sent raisins and other foods to David. (I Samuel 25:18) When David's men found an Egyptian in the field they gave him figs and raisins to revive him. (I Samuel 30:12) At the time the tribes of Israel came to make David king they brought raisins. (I Chronicles 12:40)

Outside the Bible raisins appear in texts from every important country. Around 2000 B.C. there are records of Cretan raisins being imported into Egypt. An Akkadian ritual of approximately 250 B.C. calls for raisins "from the land of Tilmun" to be used in sacrifices to the deities of the city of Uruk. Hannibal relied on raisins for sustenance when he crossed the Alps into Italy 200 years before Christ. Cleopatra, who was born in 69 B.C., appeased Mark Anthony by gathering the rarest varieties of raisins for him. In Rome raisins were so highly regarded that slaves were scarcely allowed to eat even those of the poorest quality.

As food, medicine, a sacrificial item and even as necklaces, raisins have been important to man for thousands of years. And so they are today except that now the biggest producing country is the *New* World, the United States. The San Joaquin valley in California annually produces more raisins than all the rest of the world combined.

Not every type of grape can be made into raisins. About three varieties appear on grocers' shelves. But far above them all is the Thompson seedless. This is the familiar light-green grape that we enjoy so much fresh. About 95% of the raisins produced in the San Joaquin valley are made from this delicate grape that had its beginnings in Turkey where it is known as the Sultanina. The other two principal raisins are Muscats and Sultanas. Muscats actually were the first raisins produced in California. They are a large, sweet raisin that can now be purchased with its seeds removed. Sultanas have a tart flavor that makes them especially desirable in baked goods like mince pie.

Raisins are about 64% pure, natural fruit sugar. No wonder the Romans and other people of Bible days used them for sweetening. The 2,000 year old cookbook of Apicius is loaded with raisins in recipes. One, for instance, calls for cabbage with raisins. If you'd like to try that combination—which we guarantee you is delicious—just toss a handful of raisins into cabbage when you're frying it. Or, prepare the following delectable dish.

CABBAGE ROLLS WITH RAISINS

1½ cups raisins
1 lb. lean beef, ground
1 cup rice, cooked
1 small onion, chopped
2 tsp. salt
½ tsp. turmeric
4 tbs. water
12 large, outside leaves of cabbage
1 can (10½ oz.) beef broth
¼ cup catsup
1 tbs. vinegar
1 tbs. cornstarch

Combine one cup of the raisins with the beef, rice, onions, salt, turmeric and water. Cover cabbage leaves with hot water and simmer for just 2 minutes. Drain, trim off thick portions from base of leaves. Spoon meat filling onto center of leaves, fold in sides, roll them up and hold together with toothpicks. Place in heavy pan. Add beef broth. Cover. Simmer 30 minutes. Remove cabbage rolls and keep warm. Add enough water to make ¾ cup liquid in pan. Add catsup, vinegar, cornstarch and remaining raisins. Cook and stir until clear. Then return the cabbage rolls and cook 5 minutes. Makes 6 servings.

CRETAN CAKE

½ cup raisins, ground or chopped fine
½ cup brown sugar, firmly packed
¼ cup butter or margarine
1 egg
1 tbs. molasses
½ cup sour milk
½ tsp. soda
½ tsp. cinnamon
½ tsp. cloves
1 cup flour
¼ tsp. salt

Cream sugar and butter. Add egg and stir well. Add raisins and molasses. Mix thoroughly. Stir soda into milk and add alternately with dry ingredients sifted together. Bake in a 9″ square pan at 325° for about 30 minutes. Serve warm with lemon sauce.

LEMON SAUCE

1 cup sugar
1 tbs. butter or margarine
1 cup water
1½ tbs. cornstarch
2 tbs. lemon juice
1 tsp. lemon rind, grated

Put sugar, butter, water and cornstarch in a saucepan and bring to a boil. Cook over low heat, stirring constantly until sauce thickens, about 5 minutes. Remove from heat and add lemon juice and grated rind. For added lemon flavor use more rind. Pour warm sauce over servings of cake. Yield: 1½ cups.

RAISIN CIDER SAUCE FOR HAM

½ cup raisins, cut in halves
¼ cup brown sugar
1½ tbs. cornstarch
⅛ tsp. salt
1 cup cider
8 whole cloves
1 two-inch stick of cinnamon
1 tbs. butter or margarine

Combine all ingredients except butter. Cook and stir 10 minutes. Add butter. Remove spices and pour hot sauce over ham slices.

watermelons

Watermelons were cultivated in Egypt long before recorded history. Since they grow wild in Africa botanists are convinced this is their native home. By the time the Israelites were in bondage to the Pharaohs watermelons were well established as a succulent food in a land of high temperatures.

The exodus of the Jews is set about 1440 B.C. from the city Ramses that lay in the Nile delta hard by the Mediterranean. From about this same time we have Egyptian texts that extol the "melons that are abundant on the sands" of Ramses. When our own summer is upon us we can understand the Israelites' longing for those melons as they wandered in the wilderness after their departure from Egypt. (Numbers 11:5)

The fact that the watermelon is a very ancient food is deduced from the presence of unrelated names for it in Sanskrit, Arabic, Berber and other old languages. Had it been of more recent vintage it is more likely to have had *one* root word from which its name would have been derived in various languages.

Of course, we think of it only as a food but the Egyptians and other peoples have used it for drink and medicine. Among the poor, watermelon juice from an extremely ripe melon was given for fevers. In arid regions of Africa and Arabia watermelons still are frequently the only source of water. In southern Russia the people used to make watermelon beer by adding hops to the juice.

Watermelons came to the Americas with the colonists but it wasn't long before they were grown by the Indians. By 1799 tribes as far west as the Colorado River were raising them.

For summer refreshment watermelons are unsurpassed. And they have some nutrients to recommend them although none in large amounts. However, a 4 x 8 inch wedge of watermelon will provide about half the vitamin A you need per day and about one-third the vitamin C. Along with these you'll get some B vitamins and iron.

Probably the most often asked question is: "How do I pick a ripe melon?" Field harvesters look for melons where the rind that lies next to the ground has turned from white to pale yellow. And, of course, the familiar thump test is well known. If a melon is green it gives a metallic, ringing sound when thumped with the fingers. A ripe one produces a muffled, dull sound. But even this test requires an expert ear and practice. Usually the melons picked for market are ready to eat. The only time you might run into a green one is early in the season.

PHARAOH'S FRUIT BOWL

As popular today as it must have been over 4,000 years ago is this mixture of fresh fruits and melons. Everything used in it should be chilled first. Place a watermelon on the cutting board and carefully remove a flat, thin slice from the rind to make a base for it to rest on. Now turn it over on this base and remove the top third of the melon. Remove the red flesh with a ball cutter or a measuring spoon to make melon balls. Discard seeds. The top edge of the hollowed out melon can be cut in scallops with an apple coring knife.

Fill the melon bowl with any combination of chilled cut-up fruit. Include other members of melon family especially honeydew and cantaloupe plus fruits in season that may include grapes, pears, oranges, apricots, peaches, etc. Garnish with wedges of lemon and sprigs of mint. The platter can be decorated too with mint, orange sections, a bunch of grapes or any other of the fruits used.

WATERMELON RIND PICKLES

    1 cup water
    1 cup mild vinegar
    2 cups sugar
    1 tsp. whole cloves
    3 inches stick cinnamon
    1 tbs. preserved ginger, chopped

Remove the pink flesh of the melon and the outer green rind. Cut the white rind into cubes or circles of uniform size. Tie the spices in a loose bag. Boil these ingredients until they make a thick syrup. Remove the spice bag (which is best made of cheesecloth or some thin muslin) and add the rind. Boil until it is slightly tender and transparent—about 10 minutes. Pack in jars that have been sterilized in boiling water. Seal. Let stand a week or more for best flavor.

A candy reminiscent of the gum drop can be made from the rind of watermelons or cucumbers. It has a delicate flavor and lends itself to variations. You may want to make several of these—or one several times—but we suggest that you cook only one cupful of rind at a time to make it easier to handle. However, all of the rind can be prepared at once, in advance.

To prepare the rind, remove the hard, dark green outer skin and all of the pink meat. Cut the remaining rind into small strips, ¼ to ½ inches wide and about an inch long. Mix ¼ cup salt in one quart of water to cover. Refrigerate overnight.

Drain, rinse and drain again. Mix fresh salt water, as above, and boil rind for 20 minutes. Drain.

CRAZY CANDY

1 cup watermelon rind prepared as above
3 tbs. lemon juice
1 cup sugar

Put rind in a heavy skillet, add lemon juice and sugar. Bring to a boil and reduce heat to lowest point possible. Simmer, stirring to prevent sticking, until syrup is used up and rind is glassy, about 30 minutes.

Spread the pieces of rind out on buttered plates. When cool, roll each one in sugar.

Cinnamon or cloves and food colors can be added to the syrup for variation, or the rind can be dipped in chocolate instead of sugar.

4 to 6 oz. milk chocolate
1 tbs. paraffin
1 tbs. butter

Melt over warm (not hot) water. Dip the candy and place on waxed paper.

Grain, Bread, nuts

Scene from Egyptian wall painting about 3,500 years old. Workmen are winnowing grain from chaff. Stylized figures are typical of Egyptian art.

almonds

Almonds are so familiar to us in everything from candy bars to soup that it may be a bit difficult to realize they were equally familiar to the people of Bible days.

In those ancient times the almond had three important values. It was a source of food and of a highly prized oil. But perhaps most important the almond symbolized the fruitful awakening of the earth each spring. For the almond tree bursts suddenly into bloom in January in a climate like that of Palestine. To walk through a California almond orchard in February or March is to understand the delight of the people of Bible times. The trees are solid with lightly perfumed white and pink blossoms and very few young leaves.

The Lord himself loved the almond so much that he commanded Moses to make His candlesticks with cups in the form of almonds. (Exodus 25:33) When the rod of Aaron sprouted, it bore almonds. (Num. 17:8) Almond branches are known for the speed with which they will break into premature bloom if they are placed in water in a warm spot.

The Mediterranean area is still the center of world almond production. However, in the U.S. a big commercial crop is produced in California. The nuts are used extensively in our candy, baking and food industries. Like all tree nuts, almonds are high in the unsaturated fatty acid known as linoleic. But in comparison with other nuts the almond contains a great deal more vitamin B_2 as well as more calcium. So, in addition to its tastiness the almond is very nutritious.

Unshelled almonds are a popular nut in American homes at Christmas. Out of the shell, in its natural form with the brown skin intact, the almond is called "unblanched." This is the way most candy and ice cream manufacturers use them. But your grocer has almonds in a wonderful array of forms. Blanched almonds are skinless. Both blanched and unblanched nuts can be purchased roasted or unroasted, in bags or cans. Blanched nuts also come in sliced or slivered forms.

They blend superbly with a multitude of other foods. Whole almonds go well with fruit, fresh or dried, for dessert platters. A glazed baked ham takes on an elegant air when topped with whole blanched almonds. Cakes and cookies look better, taste better if they're topped with crunchy almonds. Just remember to use unroasted nuts on food that will be exposed to direct heat.

AARON'S ALMOND FUDGE

    1 lb. confectioner's sugar
½ cup butter or margarine
¼ cup cream
¼ tsp. salt
⅔ cup semi-sweet chocolate bits
    1 cup blanched almonds, chopped

Combine sugar, butter or margarine, cream and salt. Stir constantly as you heat. Bring to a full boil. Remove from heat and add chocolate. Stir until melted and mixture is well blended. Stir in almonds. Pour into well greased 8 inch square pan. Cool until firm.

Here are some cookies you can make any time and keep for weeks. The cookies are such white, delectable, melt-in-your-mouth morsels we've dubbed them:

HEAVENLY TEA CAKES

1½ cups blanched almonds
  1 cup butter or margarine
¼ cup sugar
  1 tsp. grated orange rind
¼ tsp. salt
  1 tsp. vanilla
  2 cups sifted flour
     confectioner's sugar

Put almonds through a meat grinder with a medium blade; or chop very fine. Cream butter or margarine with sugar. Mix in orange rind, salt and vanilla. Stir in flour and almonds. For easy handling chill dough in refrigerator for an hour or more. When ready to bake roll dough in 1 inch diameter balls. Place on greased cookie sheet and flatten each one slightly. Bake at 325 degrees for 20 to 25 minutes until they are slightly golden. While warm roll in confectioner's sugar. When cold, roll again. Store in airtight container. Makes about 5 dozen cookies.

ALMOND AND TUNA CASSEROLE

    1 cup sliced almonds
    1 can (10½ oz.) cream of celery soup
½ cup milk
3-4 drops Tabasco sauce
    1 can (7 oz.) chunk style tuna
    1 cup cooked potatoes, sliced
    1 tbs. butter or margarine

In a small bowl combine the almonds, soup, milk and Tabasco sauce. Mix it well. Flake the tuna meat and put half of it in a buttered casserole. Pour about ⅓ of the sauce over it. Arrange the potatoes in the next layer. Add ⅓ of the sauce. Top the casserole with the remaining tuna and spoon the rest of the sauce over it. Dot the top with the butter. Bake at 350° for 30 minutes. Serve with lemon wedges. Serves 4.

BARLEY

Bulls and ears of barley, food staples of ancient Mesopotamia, are shown in an impression made from a stone cylinder seal about 5,000 years old.

Barley was so important in the ancient world before and during Bible times that it was used as the basis of their measurements. The Sumerians, who flourished from about 4000 to 2000 B.C., used a grain of barley as their basic unit of weight. 180 grains of barley was their shekel which they called a "gin."

This seems a bit simple and archaic until you stop to think that we too use a grain as our basic unit of weight. A plump grain of wheat is the smallest unit of weight in both the avoirdupois and troy measuring systems and it is called a "grain." Our pound avoirdupois is equal to 7,000 grains. Shoes even yet are measured in barley-grain lengths. A barley grain has been standardized at 1/3 inch.

Barley was the early world's common denominator for bartering since money as such did not exist. In Old Babylonia about 1700 B.C. Hammurabi set down a code of laws. Prices for labor and commodities were fixed by this law. (Sounds pretty modern, doesn't it?) Many of them were payable in barley. Here are some typical ones: hire of an ox for threshing—20 qu (a little more than 3/4 quart; wagon and driver for one day—180 qu of grain; wagon only for one day—40 qu.

Important though it may have been as a unit of measure, barley was, above all, a food. In the Bible it is mentioned 32 times either as the plant itself or as some product made from it. When the Lord brought the children of Israel out of the wilderness and into a land of plenty it was described as "A land of wheat, and barley, and vines and fig trees and pomegranates...." (Deut. 8:8) When Ruth was permitted to glean in the fields it was barley that she gathered. (Ruth 2:17) Perhaps the best known of Jesus' miracles was his feeding of the multitude with barley bread and fish. (John 6:9-11)

People who have eaten barley bread report it is not so tasty as wheat. Most barley in the U.S. is fed to livestock or put into malt for brewing. But barley malt is an ingredient of malted milkshakes, special infant and diet foods and prepared cereals. At your grocers you can usually find pearl barley which has both bran and germ removed. You may find hulled barley and barley grits. Hulled is natural white barley with only the hull or chaff removed. Barley grits are cracked, hulled barley often used in soups, meat loaves, hamburgers and generally as a meat extender. Since you may be unable to buy all types of barley these recipes use pearl or hulled barley.

RUTH'S CASSEROLE

- 2 medium size onions
- ½ lb. fresh mushrooms
- ¼ lb. butter or margarine
- 1¾ cups pearl barley
- 1 quart chicken broth (or 6 chicken bouillon cubes dissolved in 4 cups water)

Chop onions coarsely. Slice mushrooms. Melt 2 tbs. butter or margarine in heavy skillet and cook mushrooms very gently 5 minutes. Lift them out and put in 2 quart casserole. Add remaining margarine or butter to skillet and cook onions until wilted. Add barley. Cook at low heat. Stir and turn until golden. Add to the mushrooms with 2 cups of broth. Cover. Bake in oven at 350 degrees. After 30 minutes stir lightly and add remaining broth. Cover. Bake 30 minutes more. Stir lightly to bring some mushrooms to top. Taste for seasoning. Arrange meat balls on top (see below). Return to oven. Bake for another 20 minutes.

MEAT BALLS: 1 to 1½ lbs. ground beef, salt and pepper. Shape meat into very small balls about ½" to ¾" diameter. Sauté until well browned. Add 2 tbs. water, cover and simmer for 20 minutes. Season to taste and add to casserole as instructed above.

IBERIAN BARLEY

¾ cup hulled barley
1 med. onion, minced
2 tbs. butter or margarine
1 14½ oz. can tomatoes
1 2¼ oz. can sliced ripe olives, drained (about ⅓ cup)
1 4 oz. can mushrooms, drained
¼ cup parsley, minced
1 tsp. salt
2 tsp. Worcestershire sauce

Put barley and 4 cups of water in saucepan. Bring to a boil. Lower heat to lowest point. Cover and simmer for about an hour, until barley is plump and tender. Drain, rinse with hot water to remove starch and drain again. Set aside. Melt butter in a heavy pan. Add onions and sauté for 5-10 minutes, until golden and tender. Remove the stems from tomatoes, quarter them and add with their juice to the onion. Add all remaining ingredients and stir in the barley. Simmer, uncovered for 15 minutes or so to reduce liquid. Serves 6.

BARLEY BARZILLAI (a thick soup)

3 lb. lamb with bones
½ cup pearl barley
3 quarts water
2 cups diced vegetables (like celery, carrots, onions or peas as you prefer)
2 tbs. flour
salt and pepper
parsley for garnish

Place lamb and barley in a large, heavy kettle. Add half the water. Cover and simmer for 2 to 3 hours, adding remaining water as it cooks down. Lift meat from soup and cut from bones. Return meat to soup. Add vegetables. Simmer for 25 minutes, or until vegetables are tender. Season to taste with salt and pepper. Make a paste with flour and a little water. Stir into soup. Garnish.

BRead

Original is a colored, limestone relief in the tomb of Mereruka, a private Egyptian citizen of about 2000 B.C.

The staff of life, the word of God, the body of Christ, a sign of hospitality, food for angels, a part of the Christian's daily prayer—all these things and more has bread been to mankind over the centuries.

From Genesis to II Thessalonians bread is mentioned so often in the Bible that its references fill more than a page of small type in a concordance. The very name Bethlehem means "house of bread."

Far earlier than any written record we know man made bread. The evidence is unmistakable. Man in the late Stone Age used a stone hand mill to grind his grain. It is called a quern. They have been found by archaeologists throughout Egypt, southwest Asia and eastern Europe as well as other parts of the world. At Jericho before the year 6000 B.C. querns were used to grind flour. They were among the earliest items of household equipment in man's first villages.

The original bread was probably unleavened. Some coarse flour mixed with water, or even milk, was very likely dropped by accident on hot stones or into smouldering coals. With the first bite man had found bread. However, experts believe that man parched his grain before he learned to make bread from it. Primitive grains are tightly enclosed in a tough husk. Heating makes these easy to rub off and permits the kernel to be chewed.

It is surmised that the second stage was to grind the parched grains and soak the meal in water to make gruel. Such a mixture allowed to stand for a day or two in a warm place could acquire yeast quite naturally from the air or elsewhere for yeasts are found almost anywhere including man's skin. So, it could have been about the same time that man first ate both unleavened and leavened bread.

At Sakkara, in an Egyptian tomb, bread has been found that is approximately 5,000 years old. It consists of small triangular loaves made from emmer wheat—a type still used in some cereals today. Another Egyptian tomb at Thebes dated 3,500 years ago yielded similarly shaped loaves of bread. They are made of coarse barley flour with the husks still present. The bread is dry and hard but not petrified and is now owned by the Metropolitan Museum of Art in New York.

Many kinds of bread were developed. The Bible speaks of oiled bread (Lev. 8:26), barley bread (Judges 7:13) and bread made from a mixture of grains (Ezekiel 4:9). Bread has been literally sacred to most of the people of the Near East. This is why they break instead of cutting it. They feel that to cut bread is akin to cutting life itself. "Breaking" of bread is universal in the Scriptures.

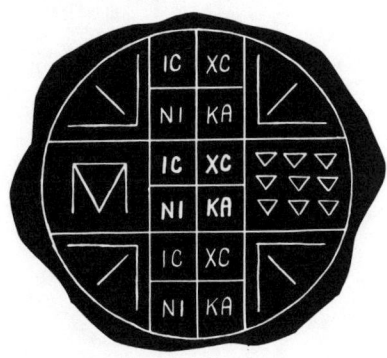

The Eastern Orthodox Catholic Church observes Holy Communion every Sunday with flat bread stamped with the design shown here. Note the letters in the center of the sign of the cross. In Greek the letters IC mean Jesus; XC, Christ. NI KA means to conquer.

Of course, baking was done in homes from the beginning even as it is today. Yet professional bakers were also an early development. In Genesis 40:16 reference is made to the Pharaoh's "chief baker." Jeremiah 37:21 leaves no doubt that public bakeries were part of the ancient scene. The ruins of Pompeii (destroyed first century A.D.) contain public bakeries where milling and baking operations were combined.

The first home-made bread mentioned in the Scriptures is in Genesis 18:6 when Abraham was visited by angels. "And Abraham hastened into the tent unto Sarah, and said, Make ready quickly three measures of fine meal, knead it, and make cakes upon the hearth." We urge you to join Sarah occasionally by baking bread for your family or visitors.

Here is a basic bread recipe that is very likely thousands of years old. You'll note that it contains no shortening as most breads do. When baked it makes a firm bread still white with a light powdering of flour on it much like English muffins. Be sure to serve it hot out of the oven. It's genuinely delicious.

BEDOUIN BREAD

1 oz. fresh yeast cake
1 tbs. honey
1¼ cups tepid water
1 tsp. salt
3½ cups flour

Dissolve yeast and honey in the tepid water. Sift in the flour and salt. Mix well and knead on a lightly floured board. Cut dough into eight pieces and shape into rounds. Roll, or flatten with your hands, until about 5 inches across and ¼ inch thick. Place on lightly greased cookie sheets. Cover with clean towel and let rise in a warm place for an hour or two. Let them rise to a thickness of ½ to ¾ inch. Then bake in hot oven (500 degrees) for 7 or 8 minutes.

The book of John in the New Testament tells us the familiar story of Jesus feeding the multitudes. (John 6:9) It starts with the line: "There is a lad here who has five barley loaves." The same story is referred to in Matthew 16:9 and Mark 8:19. The fact that the available bread was made of barley was perfectly natural in those days because barley was the grain of the poor. As such, it was probably the staple in the diets of most of the people of Bible times.

The following recipe is a barley bread that might be very similar to the one mentioned in the texts quoted.

POOR LAD'S LOAF (a flat bread)

    1½ cups barley flour
    ½ tsp. salt
    1½ tsp. baking powder
    2 tbs. brown sugar
    ½ cup milk
    1 egg
    2 tbs. butter or margarine, melted

Sift barley flour, salt and baking powder together. Add sugar. Add egg to milk and stir well. Add butter. Combine the two. Turn out on a floured board. Roll and pat into a flat circle about ½ inch thick. Place in buttered 9 inch pie plate. Bake at 425° for 15 minutes. Serve hot with butter and jam or honey. Serves 4.

lentils

One of the most renowned foods in the Bible, and what might be called one of the most expensive, is lentils. Because Esau sold his birthright for bread and lentil soup. "So he swore to him and sold his birthright to Jacob. Then Jacob gave Esau bread and pottage of lentils . . ." Genesis 25:33-34 (RSV)

A low price indeed for a man's inheritance and rights. But at least he dined well nutritionally. The food value of lentils compares favorably with sirloin steak. Lentils provide more protein and less fat. They definitely have more calcium, phosphorus, iron, thiamine and riboflavin. They also contain vitamin A and vitamin C which do not appear in sirloin at all.

Archaeologists frequently come across the remains of lentils in exacavations in the Near East so we know they have been eaten for thousands of years in that part of the world. They are referred to in ancient Sumerian cuneiform texts and were one of the crops cultivated by this ancient civilization in the Tigris-Euphrates river valley before the year 2000 B.C.

Since lentils prosper on poor soil they are raised all over the Holy Land. Soon after the wheat harvest in June they are reaped and threshed much like wheat. A tasty bread can be made from lentils, barley and other grains as outlined in Ezekiel 4:9 (RSV): ". . . take wheat and barley, beans and lentils, millet and spelt, and put them into a single vessel and make bread of them."

Lentil meal is used widely in Europe. England imports large quantities. But in most grocery stores in the U.S. they are found in the dry form and look somewhat like split peas. Lentils are an inexpensive food. A pound of them dry makes up into about 11 servings of ½ cup each. They are the basis for one of our favorite soups. In fact, you will find lentil soup often on menus in fine American restaurants.

Soup made with meat and lentils supplies all the essential amino acids. Make a pot at the beginning of the week if you want a low cost, nutritious and satisfying dish to serve the children at lunch or dinner. Heat what you need. Keep the rest frozen or refrigerated.

The red pottage that Jacob gave Esau (Genesis 25:30) is a particular variety of lentil. It is not actually red, but more of a reddish-chocolate in color when boiled. People in the Near East frequently call anything "red" that is a yellow-brown.

Biblical cookery was often all vegetables. Here's a Greek recipe that might easily be similar to Esau's pottage since it makes into a thick consistency to be served in place of beans or potatoes.

LENTILS ESAU

½ pound dry lentils (1 cup)
1 quart water
½ cup olive oil
1 onion chopped
2 cloves garlic, crushed
½ tsp. crushed fennel seeds
salt to taste

Wash the lentils and place in large sauce pan. Add water and boil for 5 minutes. Set aside to soak for an hour. Add olive oil, onions, garlic and fennel. Cook gently for 35 minutes or until lentils are tender. Makes 6 servings.

The following recipe combines meat with lentils to supply all the essential proteins.

LEHI LENTILS
(II Samuel 23:11)

 1 cup dry lentils
 1 cup leftover ham or other meat diced
 ½ cup chopped celery
 ½ cup chopped carrots
 2 tbs. butter
 salt and pepper

Wash lentils. Put in pot, cover with water and bring to boil for 5 minutes. Set aside to soak for an hour. Drain and put in a kettle with 1 ½ quarts of water and the meat. Cover and simmer for 20 minutes or until the lentils are semi-tender. Add chopped vegetables and let simmer until they are tender. Add butter and seasoning to taste. Yield: approximately 2 quarts.

LENTILS WITH GREENS

 ¾ cup lentils
 2 cups water
 1 med. onion, chopped
 2 ribs celery, chopped
 ¼ cup olive oil
 2 cloves garlic, crushed
 1 tsp. salt

Wash the lentils and pick them over. Drain and put them in a saucepan with other ingredients. Bring to a slow boil and cook 25 to 30 minutes, until lentils are tender and water is used up.

GREENS

Use 2 large bunches of spinach or mustard (or 1 of each). Wash and cut coarsely. Cook in very little water until tender and drain. Make nests of the greens and fill with the lentils. Serve with lemon wedges. Serves 4.

walnuts

Walnuts go under so many different names it is easy to become confused. The Black Walnut is native to America and, therefore, was not known to the people of Bible lands. However, it is a member of the same family as the walnut that was familiar to the people of antiquity.

The latter nut is best known in this country as the English walnut, sometimes called the Persian walnut and in more recent years in the western U.S. as the California walnut. Just to set the record straight the walnut we will discuss is the light-tan colored, thin-shelled variety found in grocery stores all over this country. Its botanical name is juglans regia.

Walnuts in millenia past grew wild as forest trees from Greece through Asia Minor, Persia and the Himalayas to China. Without doubt the nuts were eaten freely. The King James and other versions of the Bible in Song of Solomon 6:11 speak of a "garden of nuts." Recent translators have agreed that the Hebrew word "egoz" used in this context means "walnut." In accordance with this view the Moffatt version of the Bible translates this verse: "Down I went to the walnut bower to see the green plants of the Bible." Josephus the Jewish historian of the first century A.D. writes of very old walnut trees that grew in abundance in Palestine.

Theophrastus the Greek (372 to 287 B.C.) wrote about walnut trees. He called their fruit "Persian nuts." By Roman times walnuts were quite familiar on the local scene. The chef Apicius used them in sauces as well as other recipes. Romans called them by various complimentary names: Jupiter's Acorns, Nut of Jupiter or Royal Nut. Pliny gave them credit for having magical properties. For instance, "Chewing a walnut while fasting is a sovereign remedy against the bite of a mad dog, if one applies it."

The United States still imports walnuts from their native habitat in countries like Iran (ancient Persia) and Turkey (Asia Minor). On the other hand walnuts are a very important crop in this country. We in turn export them to many other countries. About 95% of our production comes from California with the balance from Washington and Oregon.

Walnuts have a high proportion of unsaturated fatty acids as well as being rich in other nutrients. In fact, a pound of walnuts would supply almost one day's dietary requirements for you. Though this is a little too much to recommend there is no doubt that walnuts are often used as a meat substitute during Lent or by vegetarians. They are so rich in flavor that in a nut loaf you will find yourself asking if there isn't some meat in it after all. Try the recipe for nut loaf below and see if you don't agree. With its nuts, cheese, milk and eggs it gives you a complete nutritional substitute for meat loaf.

KING SOLOMON'S NUT LOAF

    4 tbs. butter or margarine
    1 medium onion, chopped
    2 cups mild cheese, grated
    2 cups walnut kernels, chopped
    1 cup bread crumbs
    2 cups cooked rice
1½ cups hot milk
    1 tsp. salt
   ¼ tsp. pepper
    4 eggs well beaten
    2 tbs. lemon juice

Melt butter in skillet and brown onion lightly in it. Combine cheese, walnuts, crumbs, rice, milk and seasonings. Add to onions. Mix lightly and fold in eggs and lemon juice. Bake in greased loaf pan at 300 degrees for an hour. Serves six.

WALNUT SANDWICH SPREAD

    1 cup walnut kernels
    1 can (12 oz.) luncheon meat like SPAM
    1 medium sized dill pickle
    ½ cup mayonnaise

Using a coarse blade on the food chopper grind walnuts, luncheon meat and pickle. Bind together with mayonnaise. Spread generously on bread and place under the broiler for open-face sandwiches. Or you can butter the outer sides of the bread and toast the sandwich lightly in a hot skillet.

CHICKEN WITH WALNUTS

    3 lbs. frying chicken parts (breasts, legs, thighs)
    6 tbs. butter or margarine
    salt and pepper
    1 cup (about 8) green onions with tops, sliced
    ½ tsp. ground thyme
    1 cup light cream
    ½ cup walnuts, chopped
    ¼ cup parsley, minced

Use a large heavy skillet with lid. Melt butter or margarine and brown the chicken lightly. Season with salt and pepper. Add onions. Sprinkle with the thyme. Pour in cream. Cover tightly and simmer over low heat for about an hour. The chicken should be very tender. Sprinkle walnuts and parsley over chicken. Cover and let stand on lowest heat for 3-5 minutes to heat nut meats. Serves 6-8.

wheat

According to a tradition among the Arabs, which has been taken over by some Christians, when Adam and Eve were driven from the Garden of Eden they took with them three things: dates as the chief of fruits; the myrtle, chief of sweet-scented flowers; and an ear of wheat which was considered the chief of *all* foods.

This is legend. But we know from archaeological excavations that wheat is one of the earliest plants cultivated by man. Carbonized kernels at least 6,700 years old have been found in eastern Iraq.

Biblical translators frequently use the word "corn" in place of "wheat" or "grain." This is due to the fact that wheat fields in the Old World still are called "corn" fields. But "wheat" or grain in general is what is meant. Indian maize, called corn in the U.S. was not known in Biblical lands because it is native to the New World.

In Bible days, as might be expected, wheat often spoiled in the granary between harvests. So, sometime early in man's history he discovered how to make what may be the first "processed" food. He found that wheat could be boiled to kill insects and their eggs, then sun dried to preserve it until his next crop. Wheat so prepared and cracked is known as bulgur (also spelled bulgor, boulgor, boulgur, boulghour, burgul, burghul, burghol in Arabic, trigor in Spanish).

Although it has been a staple in the Near East for thousands of years, bulgur is relatively unknown in America except to immigrants from lands like Lebanon, Syria, Armenia, etc. Yet this very year the U.S. will produce over 400,000,000 pounds of bulgur for shipment to more than 100 countries.

In cookery bulgur can be used almost the same as cracked wheat. The principle differences are that bulgur keeps much better and cooks more quickly at lower temperatures than cracked wheat. Bulgur is known to gourmets as the primary ingredient in pilaf (also spelled pilau and pilav. Pilaf is made of rice, too). Most fancy food stores feature bulgur pilaf at fancy prices. Yet bulgur can be purchased for as little as 15c a pound in stores that carry it.

If you make your own pilaf you should use bulgur or rice to produce a gourmet dish. But in the recipes below you will get identical taste results with cracked wheat in case you cannot find bulgur.

HOW TO COOK BULGUR OR CRACKED WHEAT

Use 1 cup bulgur (medium or coarse grind) to 2 cups of water and ¼ tsp. salt. Combine in pan, bring to boil, cover and let simmer until water is absorbed, about 15 minutes. With cracked wheat use the same proportions but cook it longer, about 25 to 30 minutes or until the water is absorbed. Cooked this way with an extra ¾ cup of water, it makes an excellent hot breakfast cereal.

Cracked wheat has a little nuttier taste and slightly crunchier texture than bulgur but makes little difference in these recipes:

WHEAT-MEAT LOAF

- 1 egg
- ½ cup milk
- 1 small onion, chopped
- 2 tbs. tomato puree or catsup
- 1 tsp. salt
- ¼ tsp. pepper
- 1 cup cooked bulgur or cracked wheat
- 1 pound ground beef

Beat egg lightly. Add milk. Stir. Add onion, tomato puree, seasonings and bulgur. Stir again. Add beef. Work it together and shape into a loaf. Bake one hour in shallow pan at 325 degrees. Serves 4 to 6. An excellent way to use left-over bulgur or cracked wheat; but the loaf is so good it's worth the few minutes extra to cook them fresh.

WHEATEN STUFFING (for poultry or game)

- ½ cup margarine or butter
- ½ cup onion, chopped
- ½ cup celery, chopped
- ½ cup apple, peeled, cored and chopped
- giblets chopped
- 2½ cups cooked bulgur or cracked wheat
- ½ cup almonds, blanched and slivered
- 1 tsp. salt
- ¼ tsp. pepper
- ½ tsp. poultry seasoning

Boil giblets for about an hour in just enough water to cover. Save this stock for gravy. Melt margarine or butter in heavy skillet, add onion, celery, apple and giblets. Sauté until the onions are lightly browned. Blend in bulgur, almonds and seasonings.

Whole grains of wheat with only the chaff removed are sometimes called "wheat berries." Especially selected red wheat from Montana and South Dakota is best. It makes a very tasty, certainly a nutritious, breakfast cereal. Wheat berries are available in most specialty food stores, are easily cooked and keep well in the refrigerator after cooking.

WHEAT-BERRY CEREAL

1 cup whole cereal wheat
2½ cups water
1 tsp. salt

Bring to a good boil in top of a double boiler. Place over boiling water. Reduce heat to lowest point and steam for about 3 hours, until wheat is plump and tender. Or let it stand overnight on a pilot burner. Serve warm with milk and brown sugar, or honey.

The woman at the left carries onions in her triangular basket in this scene from an ancient Egyptian tomb.

vegetables

artichokes

In Genesis 3:18 the King James version of the Bible reads: "Thorns also and thistles shall it bring forth to thee; and thou shalt eat the herb of the field." The 20th century version by the University of Chicago, edited by Goodspeed reads: "Thorns and thistles shall it produce for you, so that you will have to eat wild plants."

The Midrash commentary on the Bible compiled by Jewish rabbis since 200 A.D. interprets the original text as referring to artichokes and cardoon. This reasoning is consistent with the facts that the artichoke and cardoon are closely related. Both are members of the thistle family and look like giant thistles. Further support to the fact that artichokes were eaten in Bible days comes from Greek and Roman source material with comments on growing artichokes as well as recipes for preparing cardoon and artichokes.

Thistle though it may be the cardoon (used interchangeably with artichoke in this book) was a very popular plant in Roman gardens. It brought a higher price than any other. In those days it was eaten for the tender leaves and young, undeveloped stalks as well as for the head or flower bud which we now relish. It was used as greens i.e. a potherb and as a salad plant.

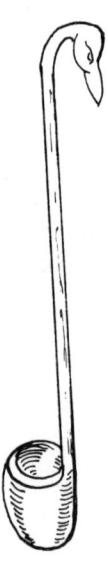

The artichoke we know is the Globe artichoke also called French or Italian artichoke. Incidentally, it has no relationship to the so-called Jerusalem artichoke which is not from Jerusalem nor is it an artichoke. Artichokes are considered a luxury in America. But their price is modest whether you buy them fresh, frozen or canned. They have been grown in America since the 18th century mostly for consumption by French and Spanish peoples who have loved them for generations. The artichoke was introduced to America primarily by the French who settled Louisiana and the Spanish who colonized California. Today these two states alone grow them in appreciable quantities with California unquestionably the larger producer by a very wide margin.

Cooked artichokes compare favorably with cooked cabbage in nutritional value with a slight edge in their content of calcium, phosphorus, iron, sodium, potassium, vitamin A, riboflavin and niacin.

You can enjoy Globe artichokes in two widely different forms. The fresh, whole "choke" is cooked and only the inner end of the leaf is eaten. It is usually dipped in a sauce, then drawn through the teeth to scrape off the edible portion. After all the leaves have been removed you will find a feathery center or core. This lifts out in one piece by slipping a fork or knife under and around it. Do not eat that. Under it is a fleshy heart which you will find quite delectable. Many Europeans eat only this heart.

"Hearts" of artichokes are also marketed frozen, canned or in glass. Some come in a sauce or marinade. These so-called "hearts" are actually tiny artichokes that have had their outer leaves stripped off to leave only some inner leaves attached to the real heart or base. We find these delicious, particularly those packed in olive oil. Eat 'em right out of the container as hors d'oeuvres or cut up in salads.

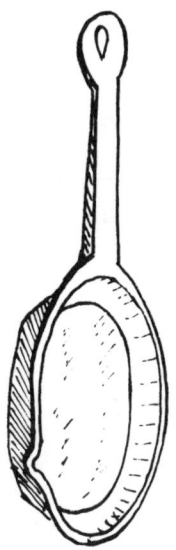

ATHENIAN ARTICHOKES

1 package frozen artichoke hearts
1 small (8 oz.) can pearl onions
2 or 3 green onions with tops, chopped
½ tsp. salt
2 tbs. butter or margarine
salt and pepper to taste

Place frozen artichoke hearts in a saucepan with 1 cup water and ½ tsp. salt over high heat. As the water starts to boil separate the hearts with a fork. Add chopped green onions and canned onions. Cover and lower the heat. Cook 8 minutes. Drain. Add butter, salt and pepper.

FRESH, WHOLE ARTICHOKES

6 medium artichokes
2 ribs of celery with leaves
1 onion, sliced
1 lemon, juiced
2 tsp. salt

Soak artichokes in cold water half an hour. Cut off stems and coarse lower leaves and about an inch straight across the top. Put enough water to cover them in a large pan, add celery, onion, lemon juice and salt. Bring to a boil. Add artichokes and cook 25 to 45 minutes until stems can be pierced easily with a fork. Turn upside down to drain and serve with melted butter, mayonnaise or Hollandaise sauce. To eat, tear off a leaf, dip in sauce and pull through your teeth as described above.

Here is a very elegant way to serve artichokes. It can be a beautiful plate as hors d'oeuvres, an addition to any buffet, a "centerpiece" salad for the family to share or arranged on individual salad plates. It's an easy dish to prepare and, except for arranging on the serving plate, a dish that can be put together in advance.

CROWN OF CARDOON

2 or 3 artichokes, fresh
1 clove garlic
1 tsp. vinegar
6 pepper corns

Wash the artichokes carefully under running water. Remove stems and outer leaves. Use kitchen shears to remove thorny tips from remaining leaves. Place in about an inch of boiling, salted water. Cover and cook until easily pierced with a fork, 25 to 35 minutes. Remove and turn upside down to cool and drain.

TOMATO CUP:

Slice about ½ inch from bud end of an especially nice looking tomato. Carefully scoop out the inside (reserve for marinade) leaving just the outer shell. Wrap shell in plastic and refrigerate until needed.

MARINADE—Place following in your blender:

tomato pulp
½ cup olive oil
¼ cup lemon juice
¼ tsp. salt
pepper
¼ tsp. oregano
1 clove garlic, crushed

Blend thoroughly. Remove the leaves from the artichoke and arrange them 'round and 'round in a mixing bowl. Discard the innermost, smallest leaves and thistle. Add the heart or base to the bowl and pour the marinade over all. Refrigerate until serving time.

To serve, remove the leaves from marinade and arrange in rows like overlapping flower petals on serving plate. Leave enough room in the center for the tomato cup. Fill the cup with a dip made from

1 part marinade   2 parts mayonnaise

This is a sharp, zesty dip. You can adjust it to suit your taste by increasing the mayonnaise. Serves 4-6.

BEaNS

The broad bean shown here as pods among the leaves was boiled and eaten as a vegetable as we do green beans. The beans within the pod were also eaten as we do peas.

If one were asked to name the universal vegetable he might well pick the bean. For beans originated independently in both the New and Old World long before written records were left. And they have remained a mainstay of the human diet in all countries.

In the ancient world, from the coffins of mummies in Egypt to the remains of dwellings in mainland Greece, archaeologists have found beans. We know they were introduced into Spain in Neolithic times and from that point spread rapidly north into what is now Europe. Small beans have been excavated in Palestine and dated sometime before 2000 B.C. The same type of bean has been found in Bronze Age deposits in Switzerland.

Around 1000 B.C. when David was encamped with his men at the place called Mahanaim, the Bible reports that, among other foods, beans were brought for them to eat. (II Samuel 17:27-28) In the sixth century B.C. at the time of Ezekiel the Lord gave instructions to make bread of "wheat and barley, and beans, and lentils, and millet, and fitches." (Ezekiel 4:9) By Greek times beans were thoroughly known. Theophrastus in the third century B.C. wrote extensively about their cultivation and noted that the white variety seemed to be sweeter than others.

Many of these references are to a type of bean unknown in early America. The people of Biblical lands ate what is called today the broad bean also referred to as fava or faba bean, English bean, European bean and Windsor bean. Although little used in the United States even now, except by people of European origins, the broad bean is the third most important bean in the world in terms of quantity produced. About 3,000,000 pounds a year are grown in this country; but in Europe, Egypt, Palestine and even Latin America the broad bean is an important food crop. Catalogs of major U.S. seed companies usually list it. Like some of our New World beans it was, and is, eaten both dried and green in the pod.

Nutritionally speaking the broad bean in its pod compares with our green or snap beans. However, it contains nearly three times more food energy and proteins than the snap bean. And its mineral and vitamin contents generally exceed that of our native bean.

Since the broad bean is not readily available on the American market but is similar to our snap bean we'll give you some recipes for the latter. Incidentally, always keep green beans refrigerated until you cook them. Otherwise they lose both folic and ascorbic acid. By the same token they retain more of the vitamin C if cooked at once in a tightly covered kettle or steamed. Wax beans may be covered immediately, but green beans should be cooked uncovered for about 5 minutes and then covered during the remainder of the cooking time which will run 10 to 20 minutes more or until tender. This keeps their attractive green color from turning to an unappetizing brownish green.

GREEN BEANS EZEKIEL

1 package (9 or 10 oz.) frozen cut green beans (or equivalent in fresh or canned)
½ cup sliced ripe olives
2 tbs. butter or margarine
1 tbs. wine (or other) vinegar
1 tbs. pimiento, chopped
1 tsp. dill weed

Boil beans in a small amount of water uncovered for first 5 minutes. Do not overcook but follow package instructions. Drain and add remaining ingredients and toss lightly. Return to very low heat until butter is melted and added ingredients are hot. Serves four.

GREEN BEANS WITH APPLE JELLY

1 package (9 or 10 oz.) frozen green beans
(or equivalent in fresh or canned)
½ cup apple jelly
dash of cinnamon

Cook the beans according to directions on package. If you use fresh ones note cooking instructions above. Melt jelly in small saucepan. When beans are tender, drain and pour the melted jelly over them. Add dash of cinnamon. Serves 3 or 4. If you used canned beans simply drain them and heat in the jelly.

FOUR-BEAN-SALAD

1 can kidney beans
1 can garbanzo beans
1 can green beans
1 can yellow wax beans
½ cup green pepper, diced
½ cup onion, diced
¾ cup sugar
¾ cup vinegar
⅓ cup olive oil
1 tsp. salt
½ tsp. pepper
¼ tsp. oregano

Drain and rinse the kidney beans. Then add other beans, green pepper and onion. Mix the remaining ingredients and pour over. Let stand for several hours, or overnight, in refrigerator to marinate before serving. This makes a large salad that will serve 12 at a picnic or buffet. Or serve it with bread and a beverage to make a meal for 6. It keeps very well when refrigerated, getting better each day, so don't let the amount involved keep you from enjoying it.

Scene of slaves working on a pyramid in ancient Egypt recalls the days of bondage of the Israelites which they remembered along with the good things they had to eat including cucumbers. (See Numbers 11:5)

CUCUMBERS

In the summer heat of ancient Egypt or modern America cucumbers have always been popular. So, it is easy to understand the Israelites as they wandered in the broiling desert of Sinai after the Exodus and their longing for cucumbers. "We remember the fish, which we did eat in Egypt freely; and the cucumbers. . . ." (Numbers 11:5)

There was hardly a hot climate in the ancient world that did not have its gardens of cukes. They were a food of royalty, as well as slaves, in Egypt for they have been found as part of the funerary remains in the tomb of Sesostris I who ruled from 1971 to 1961 B.C., a little over 500 years before the Hebrews made their exodus. Merodach-baladan, who is mentioned as king of Babylon in Isaiah 39:1, left a record of his vegetable gardens which included cucumbers. Texts from the Third Dynasty of Ur in Sumer around 2000 B.C. tell of cucumbers provided for the king and queen.

Even the gods of those days relished them. In a Sumerian myth about the great god Enki the story is told of the goddess Uttu who insisted he bring her gifts of cucumbers, apples and grapes. This he dutifully did. The date is unknown but definitely was more than 4000 years ago. The Roman Emperor Tiberius, who lived during the time of Christ, liked cucumbers so well he insisted on them every day the year around. One might almost call them a royal vegetable for kings have continued to enjoy them. Charlemagne in ninth century France had them growing in his gardens.

Cucumbers have long been used in cosmetics to keep the skin soft and white and as a soothing lotion for burned or irritated skin. The scent of cucumbers has even been added to perfume.

Columbus brought cucumbers to America when he planted some in Haiti in 1494. After that they spread so rapidly that the Indians grew them extensively. There are a number of varieties. The little gherkins you buy in glass jars are small pickled cukes. At the other end of the scale are seedless hothouse cukes that grow to nearly two feet in length.

Cucumbers for slicing should be dark or medium green, firm, bright and well shaped. Withered or shriveled cukes are tough and rather bitter. You can detect old ones by their over grown and somewhat puffy appearance as well as a dull and sometimes yellowish color.

With only 55 calories in an entire pound, on the average, cukes are popular with weight watchers. Incidentally, it is a fact that "cool as a cucumber" is an apt phrase. A cuke in the field on a hot day runs about 20 degrees cooler inside than the surrounding air. A little trick we discovered long ago is to cut a peeled cuke into one inch squares and drop it in your pitcher of iced tea. It brings a delicate coolness to the tea you'd never believe until you taste it.

As a salad vegetable they're tops. Here's a recipe for cucumbers with a sauce that uses ingredients quite popular in Bible days.

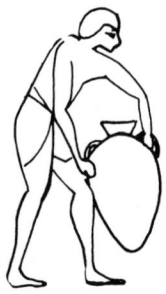

CUCUMBERS 'N LABAN
(Laban is Arabic for yogurt)

    1 large cucumber
    1 clove garlic, crushed
  ½ tsp. salt
    1 cup (8 oz.) plain yogurt
    1 tbs. dried mint

Peel and slice cucumber. Stir garlic and salt into yogurt. Fold in cucumber and mint. Serve cold in small bowls.

Here's an unusual recipe that is a gourmet dish like vichysoisse.

COLD CREAM OF CUCUMBER SOUP

    2 large cucumbers
    1 small onion, minced
    4 cups chicken broth
    1 cup cream
    2 green onions with tops, chopped fine

Peel and dice cucumbers. Combine in saucepan with minced onion and broth. Bring to boil then simmer 30 minutes. Cool and purée in a blender. Chill for several hours or overnight. When ready to serve stir in cream and garnish with the green onions. Serves 6.

TIBERIAN CUCUMBERS

    2 medium cucumbers, pared
    1 tbs. butter or margarine
    2 green onions, with tops, sliced fine
    2 tbs. flour
    ½ tsp. salt
    pepper
    1 cup milk
    1 egg, beaten
    parsley for garnish

Cut cucumbers in quarters lengthwise then slice in ½ inch pieces. Put in boiling salted water. Return to boil and cook for 10 minutes. Drain and keep warm. Melt butter in a heavy saucepan. Sauté onions until limp and golden. Stir in flour, salt and pepper. Stir until smooth and then gradually stir in milk. Bring to boiling point and stir until it thickens. Pour a little sauce into the beaten egg, stirring constantly, then add egg mixture to sauce. Stir over low heat until the egg and cream sauce sets. Add cucumbers, adjust seasoning and serve hot. Serves 4.

dandelion GREENS

Biblical botanists are pretty well agreed that the dandelion was one of the "bitter herbs" called for in the Passover meal. (Exodus 12:8; Numbers 9:11)

Support for this view comes from the Talmud. Our oldest copies of it were written down sometime after 200 A.D. But the contents date back to oral teachings that pre-date the time of Jesus. A comment by Rabbi Juhah in the Talmud is to the effect that "whatever plant contains an acrid sap qualifies as a bitter herb." This, together with the fact that the dandelion grew freely in Biblical lands long before the Christian era, makes us certain that it was eaten as part of the Passover and at other times as well.

Greek works from the fourth century B.C. list it among their potherbs i.e. greens that must be cooked before eating. Dandelion seeds have been identified from glacial deposits over 10,000 years old. As they float through the air today most of us are quite familiar with 'em.

The name itself is a corruption of the French "dent de lion" which means "lion's tooth." This in turn goes back to the Greek name for it "leontodon." In the old country it was sometimes called "Priest's crown" from the appearance of the plant when the white head is gone to leave a bald pate surrounded by drooping bracts.

As in lettuce, endive and chicory (all of which are mentioned in the Talmud as bitter herbs) the dandelion contains a peppery white sap. Consequently it is eaten only when the leaves are very young and tender. Perhaps, like us, some of our readers have gathered them in the spring and enjoyed them raw in salads or well cooked in place of other greens like spinach.

Dandelions contain more vitamin A than any other popular fruit or vegetable. For instance they have at least 50% more vitamin A, as well as more of certain B vitamins, calcium and phosphorus than spinach greens. Dandelions have long been popular in France where several varieties are cultivated. In 1836 they were grown commercially for the Boston market and are still available in some parts of the U.S. all year 'round although the biggest months are April and May.

Roasted dandelion roots are used to make a coffee substitute. They are dried, roasted until they are the color of coffee, then ground. People who have drunk it say it is remarkably similar to coffee. Of course, the dandelion has been used for medicinal purposes for hundreds if not thousands of years. The old herbals dwell at length on its application to various illnesses. Dandelion wine is still part of the American scene as it is in Europe. The dried leaves are often used in herb beers in England and parts of Canada.

But it is known best in this country as a fresh vegetable. The young leaves make a tasty vegetable sandwich with butter and salt or perhaps a dash of lemon juice and pepper. Cut it fresh into your green salad along with lettuce or other salad greens. It adds a piquant taste.

If you gather the very young plant right out of the lawn or meadow cut it at the tap root just below the ground so the whole plant is held together. As a cooked green in case you think dandelions alone may be a bit too bitter for your family, use half spinach. In this case the dandelion greens must be partly cooked first before they are combined with the spinach for final cooking. Dandelion greens take from 10 to 20 minutes to cook whereas spinach takes scarcely 5 minutes.

BOILED DANDELION GREENS

2 lbs. young, tender dandelion leaves
1 qt. water
1 tsp. salt
4 strips bacon, sautéed and crumbled
1 tbs. butter or bacon drippings

Wash dandelions in several waters. Remove roots and flower buds. Bring salted water to rapid boil and add the greens. Reduce heat and cook uncovered 5 minutes. Cover and simmer for 5 minutes more or until just tender. Drain. Add butter or bacon drippings and toss lightly. Garnish with the bacon pieces. Makes 4 generous servings.

COAT OF JACOB SALAD

¼ lb. dandelion greens
1 medium cucumber, pared and diced
2 medium tomatoes, diced
4 green onions, sliced
½ cup cheddar cheese, diced
½ cup ripe olives, cut in half
   dressing from chapter on olive oil

Wash dandelion greens in several waters. Remove damaged leaves and flower buds. If leaves are long, cut in 2 inch pieces. Combine with remaining ingredients. Pour dressing, from the chapter on olive oil, over generously. Toss lightly and serve with fresh ground pepper. Serves 4.

endive

Curly or salad endive.

Endive was one of the bitter herbs of the Bible which the Lord commanded should be eaten at Passover. (Exodus 12:8; Numbers 9:11) In fact, the Septuagint, a translation of the Old Testament into Greek by Jews around the second or third century B.C., actually says "endive" instead of bitter herbs in its translation of these passages.

The ancient Egyptians used to mix various kinds of herbs like this with mustard. Then they dipped bits of bread into the mixture before eating. Very likely the children of Israel learned this custom during their bondage in Egypt and carried it over into the Passover meal that called for unleavened bread with the bitter herbs.

Around 700 B.C. Merodach-baladan, king of Babylon, left a description of the plants of his royal gardens. Endive is included. The Bible mentions him in II Kings 20:12 when he sent envoys to inquire about Hezekiah's health and again in Isaiah 39:1. Records from Roman times left by Ovid, Columella and Pliny all tell of endive which was eaten fresh or cooked. Apicius in the same period gives instructions for serving it with onions and a dressing of oil, wine and salt.

The reason endive is among the "bitter" herbs is that, like dandelion greens, it has a pleasantly bitter taste. This very quality, however, makes it well liked in salads for it adds flavor to the blandness of lettuce. Unlike lettuce it contains more essential minerals and vitamins. Endive has two to three times as much vitamin A, for instance, as lettuce although not so much as spinach.

Endive, escarole and chicory are all related and easy to confuse. They are eaten as green vegetables either fresh or cooked. Endive and escarole are very closely related. The principal difference is that the endive has a curly leaf with deep cuts whereas escarole has a straighter, smoother leaf. They are both sold in heads somewhat like looseleaf lettuce. The heads are low and spreading with green outer leaves and center ones that are pale green to creamy white. Chicory, on the other hand, is sold in green leafed bunches and in a white, closely knit six or seven inch long form called French or Belgian endive.

Surprising to those who have not eaten these vegetables, endive and escarole along with a lesser amount of chicory account for about one-fourth of the total greens sold in the U.S. Florida is the largest producing state followed by New Jersey, California and Ohio.

We like to mix endive with spinach for cooking. The two complement each other—endive with its piquant tang and spinach with its mildly sweet taste. Here's the recipe.

ENDIVE EGYPTIAN STYLE

1 head endive
2 bunches spinach
1 hard cooked egg, chopped
2 tbs. butter, melted
salt and pepper
lemon wedges

Wash the endive and spinach carefully in several waters. Cut the bitter white stems out of the endive leaves. Stem spinach and combine all the greens in a kettle. Add about a pint of water and 1 tsp. salt. Boil gently until just tender (about 6 minutes). Drain. Place in a serving dish. Add egg on top. Salt and pepper to taste and pour the butter over all. Garnish with lemon wedges. Serves 4.

FRESH SALAD

Use same ingredients as above. Wash, stem and break up the endive and spinach leaves. Toss together to mix. Add the hard cooked egg and your favorite vinegar-and-oil or French dressing. Makes a pleasant change from lettuce and a gold mine of vitamins.

As an alternate to the green, leafy, salad type of endive is the French or Belgian endive mentioned earlier. It is white or a delicate cream color in tight knit, long bud like form. Since we seem to be unable to grow it in this country French endive is imported to the U.S. where it is available September through June at selected produce markets. Cut into a salad French endive's sharp taste adds zest to the blandness of lettuce. It may be made very crisp by soaking 15 minutes in ice water. Split lengthwise it is sometimes served alone as salad with only a French or Italian dressing. For this method choose only the very smallest endive as it will be less bitter.

You might try the following recipe first as a side dish to see if your family likes it. If they do it can be a dinner in a casserole for it contains meat, cheese and vegetable. With a hearty bread and a beverage it makes a complete meal.

BAKED ENDIVE

4-6 Belgian endives
thin slices of ham
thin slices of cheese
butter or margarine

Wash the endive and remove damaged outer leaves. Split the heads lengthwise and arrange in a buttered casserole. Top each with strips of sliced ham, then cheese. Pour melted butter over all. Bake at 350° for 30 to 40 minutes, until tender. Serves 4 to 6.

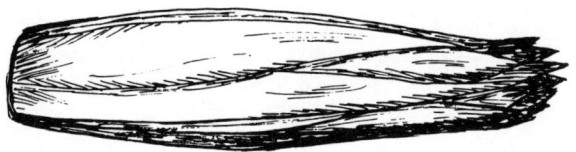

French or Belgian endive.
Also called witloof.

GRape Leaves

The grape vine was so important to the people of Bible days that the Bible abounds with references to it or the products of the vine. Grape leaves as a food are not mentioned specifically in either the Old or New Testaments. But one indirect reference can be construed as including them. In Judges 13:14 the Lord says that Manoah's wife "may not eat of any *thing* that cometh of the vine. . . ."

However, the Bible was not intended as a cookbook so we often turn to other ancient sources for information about the foods of those days. A most interesting document is a small inscribed limestone tablet unearthed in ancient Gezer which lies about 20 miles from Jerusalem. It is called the Gezer Calendar and is dated around 1000 B.C., about the time of Saul and David. In a few words it outlines the agricultural year. According to this document the pruning of the vines took place when they were in foliage. Inasmuch as people in those days wasted nothing we can be certain they ate the leaves and burned the wood.

The most telling evidence of the use of grape leaves for food are the customs of the people of Bible lands which are handed down from generation to generation literally unchanged right up to the present. From Lebanon, Arabia, Palestine, Turkey, Greece and Rome have come recipes for grape leaves—adequate proof they were long and widely used as a food. In fact, grape leaves have been eaten all over the world: China, Japan, East Indies, Asia, Australia, India and to lesser degree in the U.S.

Friends of ours make a point of gathering wild grape leaves in the spring when they are young and tender. We grow our own and use them freely in cooking. But no matter where you live now you will find grape leaves. They come glass packed in one and two pound sizes usually in brine. If your grocer doesn't have them a specialty shop should. They are essential to the preparation of a vegetable-meat roll known variously as sarmis, sarmali, dolmas or malfouf. You can use lettuce or cabbage leaves in their place but for the true flavor and aroma of this popular Near Eastern food grape leaves are best.

DOLMAS
(stuffed grape leaves)

1 pint jar grape leaves in brine
1 pound lean ground beef
1 medium onion, minced
½ green pepper, chopped fine
2 tbs. olive oil
2 cups cooked rice
2 medium tomatoes, chopped
½ cup almonds, diced
1 tbs. parsley, minced
1 tbs. dried mint leaves, crushed
2 tbs. lemon juice
1 tsp. salt
½ tsp. pepper
1 cup chicken broth

Rinse the grape leaves in several waters to remove brine. Pile them shiny side down and set aside to drain. Brown meat, onion and green pepper in olive oil. Add rice, tomatoes, almonds, parsley, mint, lemon juice, salt and pepper. Simmer until all juice is absorbed. Let cool slightly. Place a tablespoonful of stuffing at stem end of a leaf, fold in sides and roll up to tip. Repeat, using about 50 leaves.

Place a few unstuffed leaves in bottom of a casserole and pack the dolmas in layers tightly together to prevent unrolling. Add chicken broth. Place plate or lid directly against top of dolmas so they will stay tightly packed. Bake at 325 degrees for 40 minutes.

If you want to use fresh grape leaves wash them carefully after choosing ones at least 6 or 7 inches in diameter. Cover with boiling water and set aside for fifteen minutes. They should be wilted but not too soft. Stem and stuff them as instructed above.

COCKTAIL DOLMAS

　　1 jar grape leaves
　　1 6 oz. can tomato paste
　　¼ tsp. garlic powder
　　½ tsp. salt
　　¼ tsp. pepper
　　1 cup chicken broth
　　　　assorted sliced cold meats and cheeses (salami,
　　　　　　pastrami, ham and sharp cheddar, caraway, etc.)

Rinse leaves, snip off stems, stack shiny side down and set aside to drain. Make a sauce of the tomato paste, garlic powder, salt and pepper. Place a slice of meat and a bit of cheese on the stem end of each leaf. Add about ½ tsp. of tomato sauce and roll to the tip, tucking in the sides as you go. Pack the rolled leaves in a casserole, pour the chicken broth over them and cover with a plate to keep them from unrolling.

　Bake at 325° for 40 minutes. Cool and refrigerate for several hours, or overnight. If you want to give them a sharper taste, add juice of half a lemon to the broth.

GREEN ONIONS

Our familiar green onions are simply onions harvested before the bulb is mature. There is no doubt that onions both young and old were eaten by the people of Bible days. The only reference to them, however, is Numbers 11:5 when the Israelites wandered in the desert. "We remember the fish, which we did eat in Egypt freely; the cucumbers, and the melons, and the leeks, and the onions...."

The Israelites had ample supplies of onions in Egypt for this vegetable was quite plentiful according to some of the earliest Egyptian records. Herodotus, Greek historian of the fifth century B.C., noted that an ancient inscription in the Great Pyramid of Cheops recorded the expenditure of 1600 talents of silver to feed the workers with onions, garlic and radishes. This was in 3700 B.C.

Ramses, the very city where the Israelites were held in bondage in Egypt was beautifully described by an ancient scribe. He praised the richness of the storehouses and the lush vegetation including onions and chives. Since chives and onions are members of the same family we are all the more certain that onions were eaten green for their tops, as well as bulbs, just as we eat the tops of chives.

From around 1500 B.C. in the Hittite Code of Laws we find this enlightening statement: "If anyone steals one *bunch* of onions he shall be fined one shekel of silver and they will strike him with the spear in the palace."

A close relative of the onion, the shallot gets its name from the Biblical city of Ashkelon whose ruins lay on the Mediterranean coast near the present day city of Gaza in Palestine. Ancient Askalon is mentioned in eleven places in the Bible. Its namesake the shallot is often confused with green onions. However, the true shallot has a bulb made up of cloves like garlic with a very mild onion flavor. It is used, like green onions, for its fresh green leaves as well as its white bulb. Scallions are a green onion, literally the young shoots from the white onion in America today. This name too is derived from Ascalon and means "onion of Ascalon."

Practically every state in the union grows green onions for the market. You'll find them the year around although their big season is in the summer for the delightful salad days. For us no green salad is complete without green onion tops as well as bulbs cut fine. You can also use the tops shredded and cut up in cottage cheese just as chives are used.

But green onions *cooked* are a real surprise if you've never tried them. In the first recipe below you'll be amazed how much like asparagus they taste. If you like the latter on toast and find it on the market for all too brief a period you will have a new solution to your problem you can serve the year 'round.

GREEN ONIONS ON TOAST

2 to 3 bunches of small green onions (about 6 per person)
1 cup boiling water
½ tsp. salt
2 tbs. butter or margarine
2 tbs. flour
1 cup milk
1 tbs. lemon juice
salt and pepper to taste
4 slices hot toast

Wash onions and cut off tops, leaving them about 5 inches long. Add the salt to the water and bring to boil. Add onions and cover. Cook until just tender. Melt butter in a saucepan and stir in the flour. Add milk and cook, stirring until it is smooth and thick. Stir in lemon juice. Season to taste. Drain onions and arrange on toast. Pour the sauce over each. Add dash paprika for color. Serves 4.

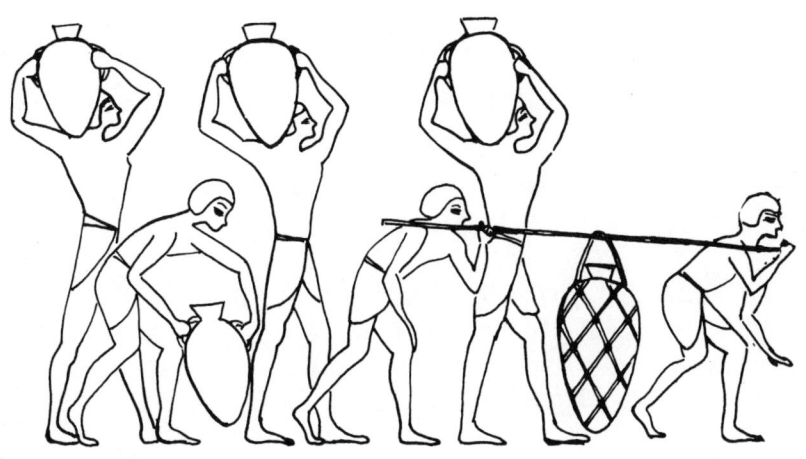

FRIED GREEN ONIONS

    2 bunches small green onions
    1 egg
    ½ cup cracker crumbs
       butter or margarine for frying

Wash onions and cut off most of tops. Cut in about 1 inch pieces. Beat egg, add onions and toss lightly. Drain off excess egg and sprinkle the crumbs over the onions. Toss again to coat them. Then sauté the onions over medium heat until tender and the crumbs are golden brown and slightly crisp. Salt and pepper to taste. Serves 4.

Leeks are a very close relative of onions. However, they are even milder than green onions. So, they are often preferred when a slight onion flavor is desired. Leeks were a companion of onions as noted in the earlier reference to them by the Israelites in Egypt. Nero, the Roman emperor of the first century A.D., ate them frequently because he believed they cleared his voice. Be that as it may they do provide a delightfully delicate flavor to the soup below. It is very close to vichysoisse with a bit more flavor.

LEEK SOUP

2 bunches leeks with tops, cut fine
4 tbs. butter or margarine
2-3 med. potatoes, pared and cut up
1 rib celery with leaf, cut fine
1 tbs. parsley, minced
2 chicken bouillon cubes
1 cup water
1 quart milk
1 tsp. salt
½ tsp. pepper
1 tsp. Worcestershire sauce

Sauté leeks in butter over low heat for about 10 minutes, stirring so they won't brown. Add potatoes, celery, parsley, bouillon cubes and water. Cover and cook for 30 to 40 minutes over low heat, until potatoes are done, adding a little water if needed. Pour into blender and whirl with a little of the milk until smooth. Return to pan. Add remaining milk and seasonings to taste. Reheat and serve hot or chill for a cold soup. Serves 4.

Egyptian slave carries ostrich eggs and hare. Painting from tomb of King Horemheb near Memphis, Egypt. Circa 1330 B.C.

dairy products

BUTTER

Men at right strain milk while man at left churns butter in scene from ancient Sumerian temple at Al Ubaid in southern Iraq. Circa 2500 B.C. Original is mosaic of cut figures on bitumen.

Undoubtedly butter came into being quite naturally long before it was recorded in history. For thousands of years milk was carried in skin bags often slung over a donkey's back. A fast trot at the right temperature would have produced butter. After a few experiences like this some bright person probably discovered the result could be duplicated by swinging the skin between two supports.

Butter is mentioned 11 times in the King James version of the Bible. But later translators often substitute the word "curds" in place of butter. The "curds" we now understand to be yogurt. On the other hand there seems to be general agreement that "butter" is the right word in Psalms 55:21. "His mouth was smoother than butter."

Around 2000 B.C. records from Ur of the Chaldees, the city made famous by Abraham, speak of butter rations for the King's house and offerings of butter. In 1500 B.C. the Hittite Law Code was set down. It is interesting to find in it the price of butter. One shekel bought a zippitani of butter or lard or honey or an entire sheep. We do not know exactly what quantity a zippitani was but it must have been fairly large to compare with the price of a sheep.

In hot climates butter obviously would not keep. The ancient solution was to heat it, strain off the solid residue and store the resulting oil. Thus prepared it is called ghee. In Hinduism ghee is one of the oldest sacrificial offerings. Ghee was well known to the Egyptians and, undoubtedly, to most of the people of Bible days.

If you've ever been served "drawn butter" with shrimp, lobster or crab you were eating ghee. It is the simplest of all sauces and unquestionably one of the best. To make it, melt the butter, let the salt and curds settle, then pour off the clear oil.

For us there is nothing like the flaky crispness of cold butter put in chunks—not spread—on bread. Maybe we're like Bontshe the Silent who is described by the Yiddish writer Peretz. Bontshe had lived in poverty all his life, but he was a good man and finally ended in heaven. When the angels gathered to applaud him for his goodness they granted him any request he might make. After considering all the things he had missed in life he finally chose "a warm bun with butter on it."

Butter is the base of gourmet sauces like Bercy, Hollandaise, Chateaubriand, Bernaise and others. Your cookbook has these recipes so we'd like to give you some thoughts that may not have occurred to you. Here are a few used by top chefs to glamorize common foods and, perhaps, to justify the prices on their famous menus.

Almond butter, featured in many fine dining rooms, is drawn butter with crushed almonds. It is elegant with vegetables like broccoli and asparagus. *Maitre d' Hotel butter* is served with hot vegetables, broiled meats or seafood. It varies with the chef but is generally: ½ cup melted butter, 1 tsp. salt, 2 tbs. finely chopped parsley or chives and 1 tbs. or more of lemon juice. One well known chef adds a grating of nutmeg for an exotic touch to broiled salmon.

Herb butter has as many variations as there are combinations of flavorings. A few ideas follow, but don't be afraid to experiment. Let your taste and imagination guide you. Work into a stick of butter 1 tsp. lemon juice, 2 tbs. finely chopped fresh herbs or spice until well creamed. If you use dried herbs take half as much.

For:	Add:
asparagus	thyme, fennel or tarragon
green beans	basil, dill, nutmeg, rosemary, thyme
beets	bay leaf, chervil, dill or thyme
broccoli	marjoram, nutmeg, tarragon or thyme
cabbage	celery seed, dill, fennel or thyme
cauliflower	basil, ginger, mace, nutmeg or rosemary
carrots	basil, dill, ginger, mint or sage
peas	basil, cinnamon, mint or savory
squash	cinnamon, dill, fennel or savory

You're familiar with cinnamon toast, of course. Butter flavored with herbs or spices is an unusual way to add real zest to the sometimes dull but eternally present sandwich. Try a bit of dill with a ham sandwich or cardamom in peanut butter. A ½ cup of grated cheddar cheese blended with ½ stick of butter and 1 tsp. chili powder makes a new taste in sandwich spreads. Spread on bread and cut in strips it is a delectable canapé when browned under the broiler.

In the final moments of cooking and serving you may discover that your sauce or gravy needs a bit more body. Or you may feel that for just a little sauce it's not worth the bother. Here's an idea that will take all the bother out of sauces.

BUTTER BALLS

½ cup butter or margarine
1 cup flour

Mix together until well blended. Roll into marble sized balls. Store in refrigerator in a covered jar. Use as needed, dropping one or two at a time into the bubbling sauce and stirring as they melt.

BUTTER HORN PASTRIES

  1 yeast cake
¼ cup lukewarm water
  1 tsp. sugar
  2 cups flour
  1 cup butter or margarine
  3 eggs
½ cup sugar
¼ tsp. cinnamon
½ cup chopped nuts (optional)
    confectioners sugar

Put yeast and 1 tsp. sugar in warm water. Set aside. Mix flour and butter until well blended. Beat 1 egg and two yolks together. Whip remaining egg whites until stiff adding sugar slowly. Fold in nut meats. Set aside. Combine yeast mixture, flour, butter and beaten eggs. Blend them well. Divide into 6 parts. On a floured board roll each one out like a pie crust and cut into 6 segments, as a pie is cut. Put a spoonful of the meringue near the wide outer edge and roll to the center. Bend the tips back to make a crescent. Place on cookie sheets and bake at 350° for about 15 minutes.

When still warm brush with confectioners sugar icing. Makes 36 pastries—and it won't be enough!

cheese

Traveler slits open animal stomach he had been using as container for milk. Action of rennet in the stomach has turned his milk to cheese.

Cheese probably was discovered long before recorded history in the same manner as butter and yogurt—quite by accident.

In the stomachs of young mammals who are living on milk is a digestive substance called rennet. To this day milk is curdled for cheese making by adding a bit of rennet to start the process. Since milk and other liquids were carried in skin bags (often made from goat and sheep stomachs in the ancient world) it doesn't take much imagination to picture a shepherd or traveler starting to drink from his skin bag only to discover the milk had turned to cheese and whey. The resulting product would have been much like our cottage cheese.

There are three references to cheese in the Bible although each time a different word is translated as "cheese." This is not surprising since we know there were many types of cheese developed by man by the time he began to write. David took cheese to the fighting men of Israel when he ended up killing Goliath with a slingshot as told in I Samuel 17. When Job was complaining about his lot in life he lamented that the Lord had curdled him like cheese. (Job 10:10)

Long before Job's time, around 2000 B.C. in the city of Ur, have been found clay tablets that refer to cheese. In one of the records three kinds of cheese are mentioned: a rare "ga" cheese which was set apart from the common curdled "ga-har" and a "green" cheese made from butter, cheese and herbs. In the tomb of a lady of Egypt who lived 5,000 years ago archaeologists have discovered a jar that contained some form of cheese. Since the ancient Egyptians made some cheese from camel's milk this might well have been her variety. Another 4,000 year old reference describes cheese mixed with cinnamon and cassia.

By the time of the Greeks, a few centuries before Christ, we find cheese was a very popular food. Runners in the Olympics are said to have been fed a diet of cheese and dried fruit. Socrates' favorite delicacy was a spiced, sweetened cheese cake.

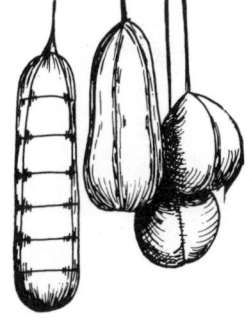

After the Greeks the Romans enjoyed a great variety of cheeses that were produced locally as well as being imported. Some of them weighed as much as 1,000 pounds. Columella, who wrote in the first century after Christ, dwells on the art of cheese making and speaks of thin cheese that must be sold as quickly as it was made, of hard cheese compressed and treated with salt for export, of hand-pressed cheese, moulded and smoked cheeses.

Like meat, milk, eggs, poultry and fish, cheese is considered to be a complete protein source which means it supplies all the amino acids needed by the human body in the proper balance. Consequently, cheese is an excellent and inexpensive substitute for meat. For Lenten cooks or cheese lovers here are recipes that are different as well as delicious.

CHEESE ROUNDS
(A Canapé)

1 cup grated Parmesan cheese
¾ cup flour
½ tsp. baking powder
4 tbs. butter or margarine
1 tsp. parsley, minced
½ tsp. paprika
½ tsp. salt
⅓ cup water
6 cooked sausages

Sift flour and baking powder into grated cheese. Add butter, parsley, paprika and salt and stir well. Add the water, 1 tbs. at a time, mixing to form a pastry-crust-type-dough. When it will ball together and leave the sides of the bowl, turn it out on a lightly floured board.

Roll it out as a pie crust and cut in squares large enough to wrap around each sausage. Place on a cooky sheet. Any left over dough can be patted into 1 inch rounds and flattened out like crackers.

Bake at 350° about 15 minutes. Slice in ½ inch pieces and arrange on serving plate. Serve hot. If you like more seasoning put a few drops of tabasco in the water.

CHEESE FONDEAU

¾ lb. Swiss cheese, shredded
¼ cup butter or margarine
¾ cup milk
¼ tsp. garlic powder
½ tsp. salt
2 eggs, beaten

Combine cheese and butter in top of double boiler. Heat until cheese melts. Add milk slowly and beat at medium speed until blended. Add seasonings. Beat as you add the eggs. Serve hot over toast. Or serve in a heated dish and let your guests dip it with small pieces of warm French bread. Makes an appetizer, entré or snack.

CHEESE CUSTARD PIE

1 pie shell, baked
1¾ cups milk
1 cup grated cheddar cheese
½ tsp. salt
¼ tsp. paprika
1 tsp. onion, grated
cayenne, a dash
3 eggs

Scald milk and add cheese, stirring until melted. Add salt, paprika, onion and cayenne. Remove from heat. Beat in eggs one at a time. Fill crust with this custard and bake at 325 degrees for about 45 minutes until custard is firm. Makes a good meatless dish or a pleasant change in place of potatoes.

cottage cheese

In the ancient world as in today's the first stage in preparing cottage cheese required cooking.

Cottage cheese is the first stage for all cheese. Of the three references to cheese in the Bible the closest to cottage cheese is Job's complaint: "Hast thou not poured me out as milk, and curdled me like cheese?" (Job 10:10)

Fresh milk curdles readily when placed in a warm spot. The presence of rennet from an animal stomach, sap from a fig or artichoke or the seeds of saffron, helps insure proper curdling. All these substances were common in ancient times. Consequently, the people of Bible days, who were without refrigeration, undoubtedly had cottage cheese as often as they had yogurt which also occurs from the natural action of certain bacteria on milk.

Cheese appears in many ancient records from Egypt, Greece, Rome, etc. Sumerian texts from 2000 B.C. speak often of cheese. The Latin writer Columella in the first century A.D. described cheese that must be sold as quickly as it is made "for it does not keep." His instructions for making cheese "to be eaten fresh" are identical with modern recipes for making cottage cheese. He tells us that after the milk has been curdled and the whey drained off it is mixed with salt and dried. Then it is ready to eat.

Even today Bedouin tribes follow a practice that must date back to prehistoric times. They pour fresh milk into a leather bag and allow it to sour. The resulting whey is a popular drink in a hot, dry climate. The remaining curd which they eat is cottage cheese.

Cottage cheese is also known as Pot cheese, Dutch cheese and Schmierkase. It is usually made from skim milk. *Creamed* cottage cheese has pasteurized cream or whole milk added. *Dry* cottage cheese is simply the drained curd without added cream. Of course, ours is made from cow's milk but it can be made from any milk.

Unlike whole cheeses like Swiss and Cheddar, cottage cheese is very low in fat content and somewhat lower in protein. Consequently its calorie count per pound is less than a third as much as these other types. Since it contains few calories plus the nutritional values of milk (in somewhat different degree) cottage cheese is popular in reducing diets. Here are modern recipes that will give you some new thoughts on the versatility of this cheese.

DELILAH'S DESSERT

   2 tbs. plain gelatin
½ cup cold water
   3 eggs
½ cup sugar
   1 can (No. 2 size) pineapple bits and juice
½ tsp. salt
   2 cups cottage cheese
   1 lemon, juice and grated rind
   1 cup whipping cream

Soak gelatin in the cold water. Combine egg yolks, sugar, pineapple juice and salt in top of a double boiler. Cook and stir until it thickens. Set aside to cool a little. Then add gelatin and stir until dissolved. Chill. Blend cottage cheese, lemon juice and grated rind and add to yolk mixture with pineapple pieces. Whip cream and fold in. Beat egg whites until stiff and fold in. Chill overnight. Serves 6 to 8. May be used as pie filling by putting in a deep graham cracker crust or a mold lined with lady fingers.

COTTAGE CHEESE WITH CURRY

1 pint cottage cheese	¼ tsp. salt
½ cup raisins, chopped	cream if needed
½ cup walnuts, chopped	lettuce cups
½ tsp. curry powder	assorted fresh fruits

Place cottage cheese in a bowl and fold in raisins, walnuts, curry powder and salt. If the mixture seems a little dry add cream to correct. Refrigerate. Serve in crisp lettuce cups surrounded by bite sized pieces of fresh fruit. Choose some to add color as well as flavor. Oranges, apricots, strawberries, large dark grapes, apple wedges with red skins left on and a scattering of pomegranate seeds make a beautiful combination. Serves 4.

Pompeiian kitchen utensil

ELAH CHEESE ROLLS (a blintz)

Batter:

    2 eggs
    ¾ cup milk
    ½ cup flour, sifted
    ¼ tsp. salt
    2 tbs. melted butter or margarine

Mix eggs in the milk then add remaining ingredients. Beat until smooth. Makes a very thin batter. Lightly butter a small (6 or 7 inch) frying pan. At medium heat place a little batter in it (2 to 3 tbs.) and tip so batter runs over the bottom to form a very thin film. Cook until bottom is lightly browned and the top dries. Turn out on a towel with the brown side up.

Filling:

    2 cups cottage cheese
    2 egg yolks
    2 tbs. sugar
    1 tsp. vanilla
    ½ tsp. salt

Dry the cottage cheese by turning it into a sieve for a few minutes while you make the batter. Mix all ingredients and spread on pancakes. Roll or fold them carefully and brown in buttered skillet. Serve with fresh strawberries or honey on top.

EGGS

Birds have been part of mankind's environment for so many thousands of years it is impossible to guess when man first ate their eggs.

Whether we look to ancient Greece, prehistoric Egypt or early Mesopotamia we find bird bones, eggshells and artistic representations of both. In Egypt over 5,000 years ago they kept geese and ducks and, without question, ate their eggs. In Crete from about 1900 B.C. archaeologists found a seal on which a rooster is shown. On the Greek mainland in tombs circa 1250 B.C. experts have identified goose eggshells.

Undoubtedly the most fascinating egg finds are those of ostrich eggshell cups from the city of Kish, near Baghdad, in Mesopotamia. They are estimated to be 5,000 years old. Ostrich eggs from Mycenae in Greece have been found with intricate engravings on them for the shell can run a good sixteenth inch thick. Decorated ostrich eggs have also been unearthed from prehistoric tombs in Egypt. The contents were eaten for an ostrich egg is delicately flavored and very much like a hen egg in taste.

There are several Biblical comments on eggs. In Isaiah 10:14 is a reference to gathering "eggs that are left. . . ." This would seem to imply that it was common practice to pick up eggs remaining in a nest. Other references in Old and New Testaments indicate thorough familiarity with eggs. A seal found in Palestine and dated from the 6th century B.C. shows a rooster, so we can be sure that by this time hen eggs were eaten there. Before this, eggs probably came from ducks, geese, partridge, ostrich and wild birds.

Most scholars feel the chicken was not known in Bible lands until after 1000 B.C. It was introduced into Biblical lands from Persia which in turn had gotten it from India. For people all over the world from time immemorial the egg, for obvious reasons, has been associated with fertility. In Persia eggs were exchanged between bride and groom on completion of their marriage contract. In Iraq some people still are reluctant to present an egg to a friend after sunset for fear of giving away a life.

Whatever the people of long ago believed about eggs we know they are an excellent source of nutriment today. Like meat, eggs are a complete protein food which means they supply all the proteins needed by the human body in correct proportions.

This food is so familiar to us all that we have decided to give you some recipes that are a bit uncommon but good to eat nonetheless.

CREAMED EGGS

2 tbs. green pepper, chopped
1 tbs. onion, chopped or minced
2 tbs. butter or margarine
4 tbs. flour
2 cups milk
¼ tsp. curry powder
1 tsp. salt
6 hard boiled eggs
paprika

Melt butter or margarine in skillet over low heat and lightly brown pepper and onion. Stir in flour. Add milk and seasonings. Heat and stir until thick and smooth. Cut eggs in quarters and add to sauce. Serve hot over toast with a dash of paprika to garnish. Serves 4.

Egyptian wall painting shows captured ostrich with second man carrying ostrich feathers and eggs.

For the Romans eggs were almost invariable as hors d'oeuvres. So, we give you here a recipe for:

ROMAN HORS D'OEUVRES

For yellow eggs:

    6 hard boiled eggs
    4 tsp. curry powder
    2 tbs. mayonnaise
    salt and paprika

Shell eggs carefully, cut in halves and remove yolks. Simmer whites for 30 minutes in 3 cups water with 3 tsp. of the curry powder added. Drain and chill. Crush yolks with fork and work into smooth paste with mayonnaise, 1 tsp. curry powder, salt and paprika. Fill whites with paste and garnish with chopped parsley or chives.

For *pink* eggs follow directions above. But this time simmer the whites in 1 cup beet juice and ½ cup vinegar. Use ½ tsp. dry mustard in place of curry in yolk paste.

EGGS VENECIA

    1 lb. chicken livers
    3 tbs. olive oil
    salt and pepper
    1 tbs. onion, minced
    3 tbs. water
    2 tbs. tomato paste
    ¼ cup dry wine
    4 eggs

Sauté livers in olive oil. Salt and pepper to taste. Add onions, cover and simmer 5 minutes. Mix water, tomato paste and wine. Pour over livers. Break eggs carefully one at a time and add to pan. Cover again and cook 3-5 minutes, until whites are firm. Serve on hot buttered toast. Serves 4.

milk

Milking scene is about 5,500 years old. Taken from a mosaic of figures on a First Dynasty temple in Al Ubaid, site of an ancient Sumerian city that lies in present day Iraq.

"And I am come down to deliver them out of the hand of the Egyptians, and to bring them up out of that land unto a good land and a large, unto a land flowing with milk and honey...." These were the words of the Lord when he spoke to Moses beside the burning bush as told in Exodus 3:8. The date: about 1440 B.C.

Time after time the Bible describes a goodly land as one that flows with milk and honey. Small wonder for the very beginnings of civilization are measured by signs that man had begun to domesticate animals from which he got hides, meat and milk. This step was taken almost 9,000 years ago around Jericho as well as in northern Iraq and Iran. In the land of Sumer, a thousand years before the time of Moses near the ancient city of Ur, a Sumerian artist pictured men milking cows, straining the milk and churning butter. From the 4,000 year old tomb of an Egyptian queen is a charming pastoral scene in which she is shown drinking milk while cows and their calves browse beside her.

Akkadian rituals of 3,000 years ago called for milk as a libation to their gods. When the early Christians were baptized they were given milk and honey to symbolize their regeneration.

Since the goat was probably man's first domesticated animal it is obvious that goat milk for centuries was far more plentiful than cow. However, mankind still drinks milk from such animals as camel, reindeer, caribou, water buffalo, zebu, yak, llama as well as sheep, goat and cow. Cow, goat and sheep milk are the most common, of course. They are all richer in fat, protein and minerals than human milk although the latter contains more lactose than the others. We can't help remarking, however, that whale milk tops them all with 22% fat and 12% protein for a total solid content of 38% versus 12.5% for human milk and 13% for cow's milk. No wonder the whale gets so big. Nor can we keep from telling you of Poppae, wife of the Roman Emperor Nero, who—before she died in 65 A.D.—kept 3,000 donkeys to provide her with enough milk for a daily bath in it.

As several human cultures have proved (the Tartars, Bedouins and Bantu) it is possible to live and thrive on a diet made up almost entirely of milk and its products. "Of all the liquids which we take for sustenance, milk is the most nourishing." Taken from a modern book on nutrition? Not at all. This is a quote from Marcus Terentius Varro, a Roman writer who lived 116 to 27 B.C. So, it is repetitious to point out the importance of milk as a food. It has been called "the perfect food." Scientists have found more than 100 separate chemical components in milk. Its

outstanding nutritional values are due to the high quality of its proteins, richness in minerals (especially calcium and phosphorus) easily digested fat and a plentiful supply of vitamins.

Milk deserves a whole book to tell of its history and its nutritional values. But any babe can attest to its excellence as a food. Jewish law prohibits the cooking or eating of meat and milk products at the same time. But our favorite cookbook from Roman times by Apicius calls for milk in as many recipes as any modern cookbook.

It is difficult to give you something new by way of milk in cooking. We have chosen, therefore, to give you something very old by taking the ingredients of one of Apicius' recipes to make an excellent modern custard. When you try it you can be sure you're eating a dessert that dates at least to the time of Christ and probably much farther back.

ROMAN CUSTARD

  2 cups milk
½ cup honey
⅛ tsp. salt
  3 eggs beaten
  1 tsp. vanilla
⅛ tsp. nutmeg

Mix honey with milk and salt in a saucepan and scald. Add to beaten eggs, stirring well. Add vanilla and nutmeg. Pour into individual molds and place in a pan of water. Bake at 325 degrees for about 45 minutes or until a silver knife inserted in the center comes out clean.

A smooth sauce made with milk can give variety, flavor and added nutrition to main dishes, vegetables and desserts. Here is a basic recipe for white sauce and a few suggestions for variety.

WHITE SAUCE

1 cup milk
2 tbs. flour
2 tbs. butter or margarine
¼ tsp. salt

Melt the butter and blend in the flour to make smooth mixture. Add salt. Add milk slowly and cook over low heat, stirring constantly, until thickened.

For a thin sauce use only 1 tbs. of flour. For a thicker sauce use 3 tbs.

CHEESE SAUCE

Add 1 cup grated cheese to the preceeding white sauce. Stir until cheese is melted. Be careful not to overcook.

EGG SAUCE

Stir 2 chopped hard cooked eggs and 2 tbs. chopped parsley into hot white sauce.

ONION SAUCE

Cook ½ cup chopped onions in the melted butter until they are limp and slightly golden. Blend in flour, salt and milk as in the white sauce recipe.

yogurt

Egyptian tomb painting depicts everyday milking tableau with one man holding the cow's calf while the cow is being milked.

For a food whose origin is so ancient, Americans have been mighty slow to discover yogurt. Bible scholars now know that the curds Abraham served his guests were yogurt. "... then he took curds and milk.... and set it before them." Genesis 18:8 (RSV)

References to yogurt under the name "curds" are frequent in the Bible. In II Samuel 17:29 (RSV) David and his people were given yogurt with honey to help satisfy their hunger and thirst.

Early in this century Nobel prize winner Dr. Elie Metchnikoff did the first large scale research into the health qualities of yogurt. He dubbed it the "food of long life" because he found that, when taken regularly, yogurt destroys bacteria injurious to health. Since then yogurt has been widely heralded as a health food.

It is the combined action of beneficial bacteria and certain yeasts that change the lactose in milk into lactic acid in yogurt through a process of fermentation. Health counselors maintain that this lactic acid supplements the hydrochloric acid normally in the stomach to improve digestion.

At the same time its therapeutic qualities were being discovered gourmets found its piquant flavor was widely enjoyed at fine restaurants in France and other old world countries. In recent years yogurt's biggest boost in popularity has been its use in reducing diets. Most yogurt in the U.S. is made from partially skimmed milk. So it supplies the highly essential ingredients of milk with few calories. Commercial yogurt ranges from 120 to 160 calories per 8 oz. glass. Made from skim milk alone it has only 85 calories per glass.

When health addicts and diet faddists praise a food it is difficult for the rest of us to realize there are plain good eating qualities in it. But lovers of good food, who have not the slightest interest in diet or therapy, delight in the mouth watering flavor, satiny texture and shimmering whiteness of yogurt. Its tangy flavor reminds us of tart apples. Many people acquire their taste for plain yogurt as they do for olives, avocados and other out of the ordinary foods with the bite at a time method.

Yogurt with honey is a favorite combination today as in Bible times. At most grocers you'll find yogurt plain or sweetened and mixed with strawberry, vanilla, orange, lemon and other popular flavors. A favorite salad dressing with us is the juice of $\frac{1}{2}$ lemon, a clove of crushed garlic and $\frac{1}{2}$ cup (4 oz.) of plain yogurt salted to taste.

Try yogurt as a beverage by mixing with equal parts of orange, pineapple or grape juice. If you like buttermilk a healthful replacement is a glass of plain yogurt well stirred with a dash of salt. A friend of ours swears a gentleman he knows in Turkey is 138 years old and attributes his longevity to his daily glass of salted yogurt.

It's fun to make yogurt at home for then you know it's fresh and you can learn to control the degree of tartness. Yogurt "starter" is available in most health food stores. But you can start it with plain yogurt from the dairy section of your market.

To make Yogurt:

    1 quart of milk
    2 tbs. yogurt, plain

Bring milk to a full boil. Set aside to cool to lukewarm. (115° on your thermometer or "warm" on your wrist.) Stir a little of the warm milk into the yogurt, then combine and stir. Pour into glass jars, cover and set into a kettle of warm water with level below jar lips.

The secret is to keep the yogurt warm long enough for the bacteria and yeasts to work. Put the kettle over a pilot light if you have one, or in a barely warm oven, or wrap it in tea towels. When the milk reaches a custard-like consistency it is done and should be refrigerated. The longer it's left to work after the custard stage the more tart it becomes. Don't forget to save the last of the yogurt as a "starter" for your next batch.

If you've felt yogurt is only for eating "as is" here are two recipes that reveal its place in cooking.

BEEF YOGANOFF

- 1½ lb. round steak
- flour for dredging
- 4 tbs. butter or margarine
- ½ lb. sliced mushrooms
- ½ tsp. basil
- ½ cup (4 oz.) yogurt
- 2 scant tbs. honey
- salt, pepper, paprika

Cut round steak in ½ inch strips. Dredge with flour. Pound until thin. Cut into 1 inch wide strips. Melt part of butter in heavy pan and sauté beef over hot flame a little at a time. Turn to brown evenly. Remove to another pan to keep warm. When all beef is well browned add remaining butter to cooking pan. Sauté mushrooms in it. Return beef. Season with salt, pepper, paprika, basil. Stir in yogurt and honey. Heat but do not boil. Serve hot over cooked rice or noodles. Serves 6.

YOGURT LEMON CAKE

3 eggs
1 cup sugar
1 cup (8 oz.) plain yogurt
1 tsp. grated lemon rind
1 cup flour
1 tsp. baking powder
For syrup: 1 cup sugar

Beat eggs. Add sugar and beat until smooth. Stir in yogurt and lemon rind. Sift flour and baking powder together and stir in until smooth. Bake 35 minutes in 8 inch square pan at 375 degrees. Make a syrup by boiling 1 cup sugar and 1¼ cups water. Use medium heat. Stir constantly until it turns to a thin syrup—about 10 to 15 minutes. Pour over the hot cake. Let stand until syrup is absorbed. Chill and top with whipped cream or lemon or strawberry flavored yogurt. Serves 8.

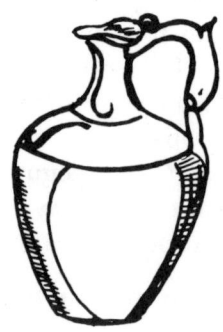

sweets, spice, seasonings

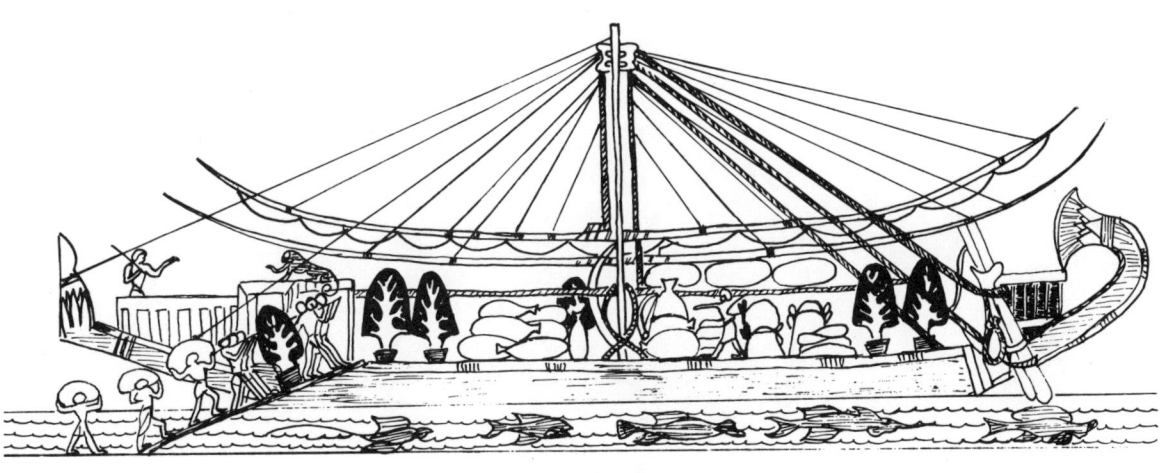

In Queen Hatshepsut's temple at Thebes, Egypt is this carving.
An inscription above the ship tells that it is being loaded at Punt
with myrrh-resin, ebony, ivory, green gold of Emu, apes, monkeys and
cinnamon wood. 15th century B.C.

Bay Leaves

"I have seen the wicked in great power, and spreading himself like a green bay tree." (Psalms 37:35 King James Bible)

Botanical authorities on Biblical plants are convinced the King James version is correct although later Bible translations give a different rendering for this verse. There is no doubt the bay tree, also called sweet bay, bay laurel and laurel, is native to the Mediterranean from southern Europe into Greece and Palestine. Travelers in

the Holy Land report it is not common there but does grow on Mt. Carmel and around Hebron. It is likely that David in the Psalms chose it as a symbol of prosperity since the bay tree is an evergreen that grows to an impressive height of 40 to 60 feet with glossy leaves and a spicy **fragrance.**

Certainly in Greek days it was one of the best known trees. So highly was it regarded then that wreaths of laurel were used to crown the winners in the Pythian contests. It was a mark of distinction too for high officials who wore it or carried its branches. The great god Apollo claimed it as his favorite. According to legend he was in love with the nymph Daphne who spurned his love. When he pursued her she was changed into a bay tree.

The Romans used bay leaves in their cooking. In fact, they often baked their wedding cakes on beds of laurel leaves. They also believed it gave oracles the power of prophecy. The Roman Emperor Tiberius who ruled during Jesus' time wore a wreath of laurel leaves to protect him from lightning storms.

Today we still import bay leaves from Mediterranean countries like Greece and Turkey although some now come from California. In some parts of the southern U.S. the laurel tree is grown in tubs for it makes a handsome plant.

The bay leaf certainly is endowed with "great power" for as a spice it is easy to over-use. Often when a recipe calls for a bay leaf, half a leaf is better. The flavor is highly pungent. Too much of it lends a metallic taste to food; but just the right amount will "pick-up" many meat and fish dishes, stews, soups and sauces.

If you'd like to use bay leaves more than you have in the past just try one inch of bay leaf in your bean or split pea soup. Or use about $\frac{1}{8}$ tsp. of the cracked leaf in your barbecue sauce. It's a standby in our kitchen. Here are recipes that are not nearly so good without bay leaf.

SHRIMP ESPANOL

1 tbs. green pepper, chopped
1 tbs. onion, chopped
3 tbs. olive oil
2 cups canned tomatoes
2 (8 oz.) cans tomato sauce
¼ tsp. celery seed
1 small bay leaf, broken fine
1 clove garlic, crushed
1 tbs. parsley, chopped
2 lb. cleaned shrimp, cooked in advance

Sauté green pepper and onion in olive oil for about 3 minutes. Add all other ingredients except shrimp. Simmer over low heat for 2 hours. Add shrimp just before serving and heat. Serve over rice. Makes 8 servings. If you buy canned shrimp it will already be cooked. For fresh shrimp you will find preparation and cooking instructions in any cookbook.

MARINADE FOR BUDGET STEAKS

1 cup hot water
2 tbs. tomato paste
1 tsp. salt
1 or 2 garlic cloves, crushed
¼ cup vinegar, preferably wine vinegar
¼ tsp. pepper.
⅛ tsp. bay leaf, crushed
2 tbs. salad oil

Mix all above ingredients well and pour over chuck, flank or other budget priced steak in a glass pan or bowl. Let stand for several hours at room temperature or overnight in refrigerator turning several times. Drain steak and barbecue or fry using remaining marinade for basting. Makes enough for about one and a half pounds of steak.

In the Book of Genesis 27:3-7 is the story of Rebecca deceiving Isaac with a "tasty dish" made with meat from the flock instead of the wild game he had asked for. The following recipe might be much the same as the one served that day.

REBECCA'S "TASTY DISH"

- 3 lbs. lamb, boned
- 1 clove garlic, crushed
- 2-3 medium onions, chopped fine
- 1 cup wine vinegar
- 1 cup water
- 10-12 whole peppercorns
- 1 tbs. salt
- 2-3 bay leaves
- 1 tsp. caraway seeds
- 1 tbs. sugar
- 3 tbs. oil for browning meat

Place the lamb in a glass or earthenware bowl. Add onions and garlic. Combine remaining ingredients, except oil, in a saucepan and bring to a full boil. Pour over lamb and refrigerate 12 to 24 hours. Remove lamb from liquid, pat dry with paper towels. Put oil in a heavy pan and brown meat on all sides. Add liquid and cover. Let simmer over low heat for about 2 hours, or until tender. Serves 6-8.

CINNAMON, CASSIA

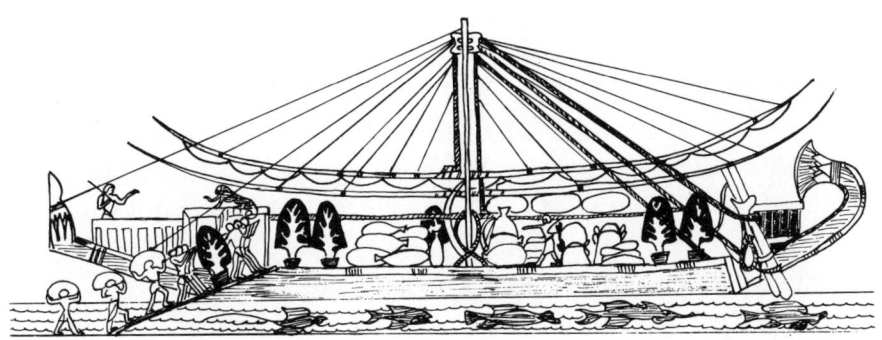

The difference between cassia and cinnamon is slight. However, the ancients did make a distinction. The fact is that most of the spice we buy as "cinnamon" is actually cassia. They both come from trees that are members of the laurel family although there is a botanical difference.

From Exodus to Revelation the Bible refers to cinnamon or cassia. When the Lord told Moses how to prepare the anointing oil He called for cinnamon. (Exodus 30:23)

Anyone in Bible days who sought a sweet smell invariably included cinnamon along with myrrh and frankincense. (Proverbs 7:17; Song of Solomon 4:14).

Over 4,000 years ago the Sumerians used cassia. Some of their records refer to cheese flavored with cassia for the king. Egyptian papyrii from the tomb of Rameses III (1198 to 1166 B.C.) tell of his offerings of cinnamon to the gods. Before him, around 1500 B.C., the Egyptian queen Hatshepsut sent an expedition of ships to the land of Punt, which is presumed to be present day Ethiopia. There the records tell us they brought aboard exotic goods including cinnamon wood. By piecing together evidence from several sources we have discovered that cinnamon and cassia were coming from countries even further off.

A fairly steady trade had been built up by Arabs and the people of India with spices from Ceylon and India. Ships docked regularly in south Arabian ports, Somaliland and Ethiopia at least as early as 1500 B.C. and probably before that. But the Arabs guarded this secret jealously. As late as the Greek period the Arabs had the rest of the world convinced they gathered the cinnamon and cassia from valleys full of ferocious beasts and poisonous serpents.

Consequently all trade in precious spices came by land or sea through southern Arabia, the domain of the Queen of Sheba.

That cassia was known far earlier than 2000 B.C. is attested by a Sumerian myth set in the land of Dilmun, the present day island of Bahrein in the Persian Gulf. There, in the dwelling place of their ancestors, cassia is said to have been created by the goddess Ninhursag from the god Enki.

The reason most of our spice cans labelled "Cinnamon" contain cassia is because the latter has a stronger flavor which is generally preferred in the U.S. over the lighter colored, more delicately scented true cinnamon.

One of the principal sources for U.S. imports of cassia is a place very much in the news, South Vietnam. Saigon cassia, as it is called, is the variety from which the best ground cinnamon is made. It is warm with a pungently sweet taste and the pleasant aroma we love so dearly in our cookery. Cinnamon is our most widely used spice in baking; but it fits into practically any part of your menu. Here is a luscious summer time recipe plus some new thoughts for use of a very old spice.

Cinnamon twig with flowers

SOLOMON'S CINNAMON CANTALOUPE

- 1 medium size cantaloupe
- 1 cup fruit juice or syrup from canned or cooked fruit
- 8 whole cloves
- ¼ cup brown sugar
- ¼ cup white vinegar
- 1 piece (1 inch stick) cinnamon
- 2 tsp. crystallized ginger, chopped

Remove rind and seeds from cantaloupe. Cut into bite size wedges. Place in glass jar. Combine remaining ingredients in sauce pan and simmer 15 minutes. Pour over cantaloupe and cool. Chill overnight in refrigerator. Serve cold.

AEGEAN ISLAND STEW

2 lbs. lean beef, cut for stew	2 tbs. wine vinegar
1 tsp. salt	1 can (6 oz.) tomato paste
½ tsp. pepper	1 tbs. brown sugar
½ cup (¼ pound) butter or margarine	1 clove garlic, minced
	1 bay leaf
2 lbs. small onions, peeled	½ tsp. cloves
¼ cup red wine	1 2 inch cinnamon stick

Season the meat with salt and pepper. Melt butter in a heavy pan and add meat, turning it with a spoon to coat each piece. Place onions in pan over meat. Mix wine, vinegar, tomato paste, sugar and garlic and pour over meat and onions. Add bay leaf, cloves and cinnamon stick. Cover tightly and place over low heat. Let simmer for 2½ to 3 hours, without stirring, until meat is very tender. Sauce may be thickened with butter balls (see recipe in chapter on butter) when you serve it. Serves 6.

CINNAMON SUGGESTIONS

ICE CREAM: blend 2 tsp. cinnamon into 1 pint slightly softened vanilla ice cream. Refreeze in an ice tray. Serve with chocolate syrup.

VEGETABLES: sprinkle over squash you are ready to bake, or add to the melting butter that goes over spinach or peas.

STEWED FRUIT: add an inch long piece of stick cinnamon to apples for apple sauce as well as prunes, pears, peaches, etc.

MEAT: try a little cinnamon sprinkled over your pork chops next time you cook them. Add a teaspoonful to the glaze for ham. A dash in chili is delightful.

CORIANDER

Spices played many roles in Bible days. They were used as condiments, gifts and in medicine. They were important in religion, too, for we are told in Exodus 25:6 that spices are called for in the anointing oil and incense.

Coriander is one of the oldest. It is mentioned twice in the Bible both times as compared with manna: "Now the house of Israel called its name manna; it was like coriander seed, white and the taste of it was like wafers made with honey." Exodus 16:31 (RSV) The other reference is Numbers 11:7.

We know that Moses was familiar with it. Coriander also appears in Egyptian writings around 1000 B.C. It grows profusely in the Holy Land and wild in Egypt as well as most parts of Europe because it has been so extensively cultivated for so many thousands of years. Mentions of coriander are frequent in Near Eastern tales like the "Arabian Nights." Hippocrates, the Greek "father of medicine" who lived long before Christ, used the seeds in medicine. It is considered soothing to the stomach and a relief for gas. To this day it is made into cough syrup by the Malays by grinding the seeds to a paste and mixing with honey.

However, coriander's greatest value has always been its use as a food. The ancients ate the fresh plant as well as the seeds. The vitamin A content of fresh coriander is exceptionally high. It is also an excellent source of minerals like calcium, phosphorus and iron as well as vitamins like thiamine, riboflavin, niacin and ascorbic acid. So, we see the people of long ago ate some very healthful plants. Leaves were used in soups and for flavoring puddings and wines. A favorite drink was made by steeping the plants in wine. Afterwards the seeds were dried and eaten with various dishes. Seeds were also sprinkled on bread, cakes and pastry and eaten with fish and meats, put in stews and ground up with grain to make a more palatable flour.

Most coriander in the U.S. comes from Morocco. Modern American spice houses supply it in whole seed form or ground. There's more of it eaten than we realize. It is regularly used in the seasoning of whole pickling spice mixes, curry powder, pork sausage, frankfurters and other processed meats. The little coriander that is grown in the U.S. is raised in Kentucky where much of it goes into the manufacture of tobacco products.

Some people describe its flavor as a mild combination of lemon peel and sage. If you have never used coriander in cooking you can try it by putting 1 tsp. in your favorite apple pie recipe. Here are other recipes you'll find make superb eating.

SERAPHIM PUDDING

1½ cups bread crumbs
1 cup milk
2 eggs
2 tbs. butter
½ cup sugar
1 tsp. vanilla
1½ tsp. grated lemon rind
½ tsp. coriander, ground
¼ tsp. cloves, ground
½ cup shredded walnuts
½ cup raisins
2 cups peeled and chopped apples
⅛ tsp. salt

Bring the bread crumbs and milk to a boil, stirring to prevent scorching. Let cool. Separate egg yolks from whites and set whites aside. Add yolks, butter, sugar, vanilla, lemon rind, coriander and cloves. Beat well. Add the walnuts and raisins. Stir apples in. Beat egg whites and salt until stiff and fold in. Bake in oiled dish at 375 degrees for about 35 minutes. Serve warm with cream. Makes 6 helpings.

Young coriander plants are marketed under the name "cilantro" when they are 4 to 8 inches tall. They look like parsley but the leaf is not as full or deeply cut. Cilantro is used in all the Mediterranean countries. It is an especially potent herb so it should be used sparingly but it does impart a unique flavor to many foods.

DAMASCUS CHICKEN

1 frying chicken
1 minced onion
4 tbs. butter
1 tbs. ground coriander
1 tsp. salt
½ tsp. turmeric
½ tsp. chili powder
1 tbs. lime or lemon juice

Cut the chicken into serving pieces and toss the onions over it. Let stand for half an hour. Melt the butter in a heavy pan and stir in coriander, salt, turmeric and chili powder. Add the chicken and onion and brown lightly. Add about ⅓ cup of water and cover tightly. Reduce heat and let simmer for about 40 minutes or until chicken is tender. Stir in the lime or lemon juice just before serving.

PORK MEDITERRANEE

4 large pork chops (or slices of pork tenderloin)
2 tbs. cooking oil
¾ cup dry wine (sherry)
1½ tsp. ground cumin
3 or 4 cloves crushed garlic
1 tsp. salt
pepper
½ lemon, sliced
2 tbs. cilantro, minced

Brown the pork in the oil in a heavy skillet. Combine ½ cup wine, cumin, garlic, salt and pepper and pour over the pork. Cover and simmer 25 minutes. Combine ¼ cup wine, lemon slices and cilantro and pour over. Simmer, turning the meat several times, for 10 minutes. Remove meat to serving dish, thicken sauce and pour over it. Serves 4.

cumin

Twice in the Bible cumin is mentioned. ". . . fitches are beaten out with a staff, and the cumin with a rod." (Isaiah 28:27) ". . . ye pay tithe of mint and anise and cumin. . . ." (Matthew 23:23) There are other ancient mentions of it. Theophrastus, the Greek writer who died about 287 B.C., covered its propagation extensively.

If cumin sounds unfamiliar to you the chances are nonetheless good that you have eaten it. For instance, cumin is used in flavoring saurkraut, chili powder, sausage, curry powder, pickles and chutney. It is a very important spice in Chinese, Spanish and Mexican cookery.

The uses of cumin have been surprisingly regional. For instance, the Germans have used it almost entirely for flavoring saurkraut whereas the Dutch and Swiss put it in their cheese. The Jews liked cumin in their unleavened bread but the Egyptians sprinkled the seeds on top. In ancient times cumin from Ethiopia was considered best with Egyptian cumin second. Now most of our cumin comes from Iran, Turkey and India.

The flavor of cumin is reminiscent of carraway seed which it resembles somewhat in appearance. In Roman cookery its use was spread over so many foods that cumin might almost be considered their most important spice. They called for it in a sauce on oysters and shellfish, in sausage, added to cooking water for beets and cabbages, as part of the dressing on lettuce, boiled with artichokes, to flavor pork, in barley soup, with lentils, peas, beans, in sauce for fowl, in stews, for roasts, in meat sauces, for truffles, with snails, on boar, venison, lamb, rabbit and all types of fish.

Extensive as this list may seem the fact is that cumin still remains a ubiquitous seasoning. It's great as a whole seed for sprinkling on bread sticks or toasted crackers. Put a few on sugar cookies and crush 3 or 4 seeds in your fruit pie. Add ½ teaspoonful to your sauces for roast pork or beef. If you make chili be sure to add an extra teaspoonful to your chili powder. Making a sauce for baked or broiled fish? Then add a ¼ tsp. of cumin. When you're cooking dry beans, beets, carrots or lentils be daring. Add a few whole seeds to the water. For a new touch in scrambled eggs use a sprinkle of ground cumin. The list is long: barbecue sauce, salad dressings, or for potato salad. In practically any soup a pinch of cumin will give it a new fillip hard to detect but delicious to taste. And, of course, it's a "natural" in stews, soups and casseroles.

For us spaghetti sauce would not be worthwhile without a generous flavoring of cumin. Here's our favorite:

SPAGHETTI SAUCE COMINO

- 1 large onion, chopped
- 1 large rib celery, chopped
- 1 lb. lean ground beef
- 1 lb. Italian sausage
- 2 cloves garlic, minced
- 2 tbs. olive oil
- 1 tbs. cumin
- 1 tbs. oregano
- 1 tsp. sweet basil
- 1 tsp. salt
- ⅛ tsp. pepper
- 1 large (28 oz.) can tomatoes
- 2 small (6 oz.) cans tomato paste

In a large, heavy pan brown onions and celery lightly in the olive oil. Add ground beef, sausage and garlic. Break meats into small pieces as you add them. Cook and stir occasionally until all are well browned. Add remaining ingredients. Stir well. Cover. Let simmer for at least an hour. (If Italian sausage is not available, pork sausage may be used; but increase by one-half the cumin, oregano and basil.) This sauce improves measurably in flavor if permitted to stand 24 hours, or at least overnight.

HAMBURGERS with CUMIN

  2 lbs. ground beef
  1 medium onion, chopped
1½ tsp. salt
  1 tsp. cumin, ground
  ¼ tsp. pepper
  ⅛ tsp. garlic powder (or 1 clove of garlic crushed)

Mix well and mold into six patties about ½ inch thick. Brown in a hot skillet. Cook over medium heat for 10 minutes or until they are done as you like them.

CHICKEN ROMANO

  1 frying chicken, cut into serving pieces
  3 tbs. cooking oil
  1 cup white wine
1½ tsp. cumin
  4 garlic cloves, crushed
  1 tsp. salt
    pepper
  ½ lemon, cut into small pieces
  1 tbs. lemon juice
4-6 tbs. parsley, minced

Wash the chicken pieces and pat dry with paper towels. Put the cooking oil in a large skillet or heavy pan that has a tight fitting lid. Fry the chicken parts until browned on both sides. In ½ cup of wine, mix cumin, garlic salt and pepper. Pour over chicken, cover and simmer for 40 minutes. To remaining wine add cut bits of lemon peel, juice and parsley. Pour over and cover for another 15 to 20 minutes. Chicken should be very tender. Remove to serving dish. Thicken juices in pan with a little flour for delicious gravy.

dill, anise, fennel

In the King James' version of the Bible, Matthew 23:23 reads: "Woe unto you, scribes and Pharisees, hypocrites! for ye pay tithe of mint and anise. . . ." This same passage by later translators like Goodspeed, Moffat, Weymouth and Lamsa is rendered as "dill" in place of anise." **Botani**cally trained students of the Bible are agreed the later translations are correct.

Nonetheless, from other sources we have discovered that both plants were known to the ancient world. Anise was mentioned in early Egyptian writings. Anise seeds have been found in Greek ruins that date to around 1500

B.C. The Sumerians of 2000 B.C. and before, left records of both anise and its sister, fennel. In the first century A.D. the Roman writer Pliny remarked that "Anise serves well for seasoning all meats; and the kitchen cannot get along without it." Fennel was used extensively by the Romans in cooking. One of their best known chefs, Apicius, called freely for dill, anise and fennel in his recipes. In fact, fennel and dill—like bay leaves—were so highly regarded they were used to crown Roman heroes. Fennel in particular was considered a sacred herb given to man by the gods to cure diseases.

All three plants are members of the same botanical family, the umbelliferae i.e. parsley or carrot family. If you look at photographs of them you will find it difficult to tell the difference. In taste, of course, dill is quite different from the other two with a pungent flavor widely used in pickling. Anise and fennel have the flavor of licorice. In cooking the two are interchangeable and are used a great deal in breads and rolls. Fennel seed gives Italian sausage its unique flavor. "Dill" is derived from the Anglo Saxon word "dili" meaning to lull, for dill water was used to put babies to sleep. It has been known since early times for its ability to soothe and help digestion.

In 1619 in America the First Assembly of Virginia passed a law that "each man unto whom a division of land is granted must plant thereon six anise seeds." So it is far from a newcomer to our shores even though it may be used infrequently in our cooking. Dill too is known to have been in American gardens before 1806.

A particular form of fennel called finocchio is relished by the Italians for its root and stalk. It is better known in this country as Florence fennel or Sweet Anise. Finocchio comes to market in fairly large quantities during the holidays and Easter. It may be eaten raw or cooked. Since it is available and because it is unusual we give you here a little known recipe for sweet anise salad.

FINOCCHIO FLORENTINE

  2 medium size sweet anise bulbs
½ cup salad oil
  2 tbs. white wine vinegar
  1 tsp. lemon juice
½ tsp. salt
    coarse ground pepper
½ cup Parmesan cheese
  2 hard cooked eggs, grated
    parsley

Wash bulbs and cut off tops. Cut into paper thin slices. Cover with ice at least one hour to crispen. Meanwhile, combine all other ingredients, except eggs, in a jar and shake well—or use blender. Drain water from anise slices and dry between paper towels. Toss with dressing. Garnish with grated eggs and finely chopped parsley. Serve in cold bowls. Makes 4 to 5 servings.

    The stalks are excellent too. They can be cut in pieces and steamed in butter until tender. Then combine with any cream sauce.

PERSIAN RICE

  1 cup dry rice
  2 cups water
  1 chicken bouillon cube
  1 tsp. salt
½ cup sliced ripe olives
  2 tbs. chopped pimento
  1 tsp. Dill weed

Dissolve bouillon cube in water. Add salt and rice. Bring to vigorous boil. Reduce heat as low as possible, cover and leave over low heat 15 to 20 minutes or until rice is tender. Fluff with a fork. Add remaining ingredients and toss thoroughly. Serve hot in place of potatoes.

A Greek myth tells how fire was brought to mankind by the god Prometheus when he was admitted to Olympus by the goddess Athene. There he saw his opportunity to carry fire from heaven to earth. From the Chariot of the Sun he lighted a torch. Its glowing embers he stuffed into a giant fennel stalk which he then stealthily carried to earth as he left.

Although it may be called "sweet anise" where you purchase this vegetable it is probably really fennel. Fennel looks much like celery with fern tops instead of leaves. It can be cooked in bouillon or salted water until barely tender, 15 to 20 minutes, drained and served with butter, salt and pepper or you might prefer the following recipe.

FENNEL ROMA

- 1 stalk fennel with tops trimmed off
- 1 clove garlic, cut in half
- 1 tbs. olive oil
- 2 tbs. butter or margarine
- 6-8 mushrooms, sliced
- 1 med. tomato, cut up
- ¼ tsp. basil
- ¼ cup water
- salt and pepper

Wash fennel and cut crosswise in 1 inch pieces. Rub the pan well with the garlic clove. Heat oil and butter, add anise and tomato. Lower heat. Cover and simmer for 10 minutes. Add mushrooms, basil and salt and pepper to taste. Cover and simmer 10 minutes more. Fennel should still be firm. Serves 4.

GARLIC

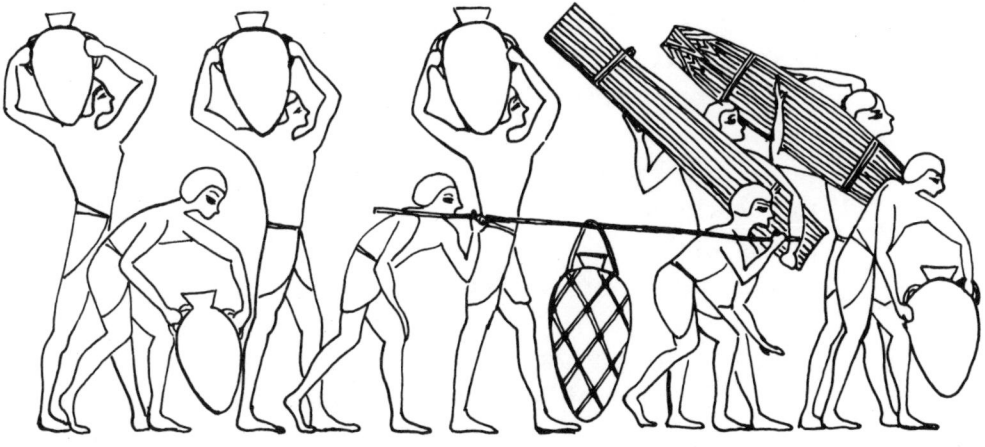

Reminiscent of their days as slaves and the garlic they relished is this scene of Hebrew slaves working for the Egyptians. From tomb of Rekhmare, vizir to Thotmose III 15th century B.C.

Garlic is to food what a pun is to conversation: delightful in small amount, but easily over-used.

Its merits and de-merits have been debated for thousands of years. Garlic was forbidden to Egyptian priests; yet in the same country men swore by it, as to a god, when they took an oath. Horace, the Latin satirist of the first century B.C., detested it. His contemporary, Virgil the poet praised garlic for its flavor. Shakespeare considered the smell of garlic vulgar. Emperor Charlemagne had it grown in huge quanties.

The only mention of garlic in the Bible is a longing for it by the Jews in their wanderings through the desert of

Sinai. (Numbers 11:5) They have kept their love for it ever since. The ancient rabbinical teachings of the Talmud call for it in many dishes and modern Jewish cookery makes an essential of it.

In the ancient East there is a myth that the steps of Satan gave rise to onions and garlic. The story goes that when he stepped out of the Garden of Eden, after tempting Adam and Eve, his right footstep left a spot where onions began to grow. With his left footstep came up garlic. The legend is not making derogatory statements about the vegetables. Rather it is meant to show the magical powers of the two plants.

Without doubt fondness for garlic through the ages has been as strong as its flavor. But each age has had its quota of those who did not care for it. The Sumerians raised it in the Tigris-Euphrates valley before 2000 B.C. and unquestionably had various opinions about its pungency. Slaves in Egypt ate it as a cooked vegetable. The Romans fed garlic to laborers to make them strong. For soldiers they believed it would increase their courage.

In many lands, from ancient Assyria to the present, it has been used to heal and ward off illnesses. Theophrastus (Greek—372 to 287 B.C.) recommended garlic to prevent injury to diggers when they were harvesting poisonous plants. I have known personally Italians who send their children to school with a string of garlic cloves around their neck to keep away colds and flu in the winter. One of garlic's older names was "clown's treacle." In this case the word "clown" was used in its initial meaning of farmer, and "treacle" in its early form of "antidote for poison." Thus, the real meaning of clown's treacle was "rustic remedy."

Like so many foods that primitive man used for medicine we now know that garlic has some remarkable properties. It contains a natural antibiotic, the 20th century word for an organic substance that checks or kills certain disease producing organisms. Modern scientists have discovered that an extract of garlic in a test tube kills tuberculosis bacteria. At the University of California, Riverside, plant scientists found that a garlic extract killed five different species of mosquitoes. Even in as low a concentration as ten parts per million they found a kill rate of 98% of mosquito larvae.

Organic gardeners claim that garlic can be planted among other vegetables or even ornamentals to keep away insects like aphids and Japanese beetle. So, it would appear that garlic has many uses beyond its primary place in our cooking.

However, it's as a seasoning we use it most. It comes in so many forms you surely can find one that fits your style of cooking. Fresh garlic in its familiar bulb is usually at the vegetable stand and sometimes with the spices. When you buy give it a little squeeze to be sure it is firm and fresh instead of hollow and dry. The bulk of the garlic produced in the U.S. is harvested between June and October. During practically every month, however, some fresh garlic comes to us from domestic and foreign sources.

Any time of year you'll find garlic salt, garlic powder, garlic chips and garlic seasoning powder. They all have their place. If you haven't added salt to a recipe and it can take some along with a touch of garlic, use the garlic salt. Garlic powder and garlic chips are used in any recipe that calls for fresh garlic. An eighth of a teaspoon is about the same as a medium-size garlic clove. They are both dehydrated garlic. Don't be surprised if they appear to have no scent. A bit of moisture will bring that out. When you use the powder or the chips in place of fresh garlic add the proper amount to a little of the liquid from the recipe. This brings out the scent and gives you easier mixing.

Measuring small amounts of garlic can be more precise than you might think when the smallest measuring spoon holds ¼ teaspoon. To measure ⅛ teaspoon of garlic powder, for example, fill and level the ¼ teaspoon. With the tip of a knife cut away and return to the jar half the amount in the measuring spoon. Presto, you have left the ⅛ teaspoon you were after. To measure 1/16 teaspoon just cut the ⅛ in half again. This brings it down to what French cooks call a "point" of garlic. We usually call it a "pinch."

To give you recipes for garlic is to fill a cookbook. The real question is "where *can't* you use garlic?" Do try rubbing a peeled, fresh clove lightly around the bowl before you put mashed potatoes in it. Try the same in your wooden salad bowl. When you season with fresh garlic pierce it several times with a knife or fork, place on a toothpick or in a spice bag and remove it before you serve the food. Never brown garlic. Sauté it lightly. Browning creates a very bad taste.

And lastly, if you want to get the pungent scent of garlic off your hands, rub with lemon juice.

honey

Egyptian bee keepers. Limestone carving from 6th century B.C. tomb of Pubes. Thebes, Egypt.

Of all the foods in the Bible honey is certainly one of the best loved. It is even compared with the word of God: "How sweet are thy words to my taste, sweeter than honey to my mouth." Psalms 119:102 (RSV)

The production of honey is almost a miracle in itself. To gather one pound of nectar a bee must tap 2,000,000 flowers. And there's more than sweetness to recommend honey. It's nature's perfect sweetener with small proportions of calcium, potassium, phosphorus and vitamin C plus traces of two B vitamins, iron, copper and manganese, everyone of them needed by the human body.

Packed into its sweetness are other health values, too. Dr. W. G. Sackett, a bacteriologist at Colorado Agriculture College found that honey destroys many disease producing bacteria. Even on a day-in-day-out basis nature has put a lot of dynamite into honey. Sports College in Canada conducted experiments to determine what quick energy foods would give their athletes the most vim. Honey won! It proved to be the best source of fuel before activity, a great pick-me-up during activity and quick energy after a game.

Isaiah 7:14,15 (RSV) tells us: "Behold, a young woman shall conceive and bear a son. . . . He shall eat curds and honey. . . ." Lo, and behold, modern research confirms that honey is indeed the perfect source for sweetening in baby formulas. Dr. F. W. Schultz and associates in the pediatrics department of the University of Chicago hospital found that honey never loads a baby's blood with excessive sugar. When honey is used in a formula it brings the blood sugar to the right level and keeps it there longer than other carbohydrates tested.

If honey was intended as a natural health food it certainly is wrapped in delectable form. You'll find it at its best uncooked. Try it "straight" as a spread on bread, toast, pancakes, waffles or hot breads like biscuits. Treat the kids with sandwich filling made with equal parts of honey, peanut butter and margarine or butter. Make Swiss honey with equal parts of honey, whipped cream and margarine or butter. Of course, it's an ideal sweetener in beverages.

Flip through your favorite recipes. You'll find many in which honey can be used in place of sugar. This is true in puddings, custards, pie fillings, baked apples, candied and sweet-sour vegetables, salad dressings—any food where liquid proportions are not critical. If you want to use this flowered nectar in cakes or cookies, however, you will get best results with recipes developed especially for honey.

After Jesus' resurrection we are told his disciples ". . . gave him a piece of broiled fish and of an honeycomb." Luke 24:42 (Latin Vulgate and Christian Aramaic. Other translations exclude honeycomb due to an alliteration in Greek texts from which they are taken.) Catherine de Medici had her fish transported from Italy to France in kegs of honey to preserve it. Mediterranean cooking often combines honey with fish, fowl and meat. Like to try this combination yourself? Here's a delicious dish inspired by a recipe in an ancient Roman cookbook written about the time of Christ.

FISH DE MEDICI

- 6 whole trout (or any fish filet)
- ⅓ cup flour
- ½ cup cooking oil
- ½ tbs. rosemary
- ⅔ cup water
- 3 tbs. honey
- 2 lemons juiced
- 3 tbs. raisins
- 2 tbs. shredded almonds
- 1 clove garlic, crushed
- salt and pepper to taste

Salt and pepper the fish and roll in flour. Heat the oil and rosemary in a skillet and fry the fish until done. Place in a shallow baking dish. Boil remaining ingredients and pour over fish. Simmer gently for about 5 minutes. Serve.

Here's a time-honored recipe from Egypt that is very simple to make. It has just the right degree of sweetness without cloying your taste.

CLEOPATRA'S KISSES

6 slices white bread crumbled
1 cup honey
1 cup sugar
½ cup butter

Heat honey, sugar and butter in a skillet until melted. Add bread crumbs and cook over low heat, stirring gently for 10 minutes. Drop by teaspoonful onto cookie sheet. Sprinkle with nuts if you wish.

APHRODITE'S SALAD

Use 6 to 8 cups of fresh fruits of your choice for this salad. Be sure to include a variety that will be colorful. You might try oranges, bananas, pineapple, peach or apricot, light and dark grapes, strawberries and a handful of dates cut in half. The fruit can be cut in advance and sprinkled with lemon juice to prevent discoloring. The dressing is also made ahead so when you are ready to serve it, all you have to do is drain off the excess juice from the fruit and combine it with the dressing.

DRESSING FOR APHRODITE'S SALAD

½ cup honey
1 tbs. sugar
grated rind of 1 lemon
½ cup lemon juice
1 egg, beaten
½ cup whipping cream

Beat the egg in the top of a double boiler. Add honey, sugar, lemon rind and juice. Place over boiling water and cook, stirring frequently, until mixture thickens. Chill in refrigerator. When cold whip the cream until stiff. Fold into the cooked ingredients. To serve pour over fruit bowl and turn gently to combine. Serves 6.

mint

Modern uses of mint are surprisingly parallel to those of the ancients. For instance, about 4,250 years ago on a clay tablet with a triangular stylus a Sumerian scribe set down fifteen medical prescriptions. One of them calls for the seeds of an unidentified vegetable, some myrrh and the leaves of a member of the mint family which were to be mixed in beer and given to the sick man to drink. Nowadays mint still is used in many prescriptions either as a flavor to hide less desirable tastes or for its soothing effect on the stomach.

It is mentioned twice in the Bible, both times in a quote from Jesus. (Matthew 23:23 and Luke 11:42) We know it grew wild in prehistoric Crete. Theophrastus the Greek who lived in the fourth century B.C. gives instructions for its propagation. The Romans rubbed it into their tables before they sat down to a banquet. A famous Roman chef, Apicius, includes mint in so many of his recipes it is hard to find a page without it. Pliny the Roman naturalist who lived in the first century A.D. remarks: "As for the garden mint, the very smell of it recovers and refreshes our spirits as the taste stirs up the appetite for meat, which is the reason it is so general in our sauces where we dip our meat."

A charming Roman myth is that the nymph Mintho was transformed into a mint plant by Proserpine who was queen of the infernal regions. As a mint plant the nymph lost some of her human traits but still attracted men with her fresh fragrance.

There are more than thirty varieties of mint found in the North Temperate Zone. Best known, of course, to us are spearmint and peppermint although all of them have pretty much the same basic flavor. Quite a few are common in Palestine today where they grow wild in ditches and on the banks of streams. The most widespread American garden mint is spearmint. It can be distinguished by its light, gray green leaves as contrasted with the bright green leaves and purplish stems of peppermint. Spearmint is also a bit more delicate in flavor.

If you have mint in your garden and plan to use it in your cooking you'll find its essential oils are strongest when it is flowering. This is the time to gather the leaves and dry them for later use. At other times the mint may be too weak for flavoring unless large quantities are used. The dried mint on your grocer's spice rack is your most consistent source of full flavored mint. In the recipes below you'll get all the flavor only if the mint is thoroughly macerated, preferably with mortar and pestle. Grind until it is fine and the scent fills the air.

Mint's a "must" with lamb either in a sauce or as mint jelly. But it lends a delicate freshness to a wide variety of other dishes like fruit salads, meat sauces, cooked with vegetables or used as flavoring in sherbets, cake frostings, etc. For a delightfully fresh addition to chocolate desserts top them with whipping cream to which you have added a few crushed mint leaves.

MINT SAUCE FOR LAMB

¼ cup mint, cut fine
1 cup white wine vinegar
¼ cup sugar
dash of salt

Combine the ingredients in a saucepan and place over medium heat. Bring just to the boiling point. Remove from heat and cool to room temperature. Serve with roast lamb or lamb chops. This sauce keeps well in the refrigerator for future use.

MINTHO'S PEAS

1 package (9 or 10 oz.) frozen green peas
1 can (4 oz.) button mushrooms
2 tbs. butter or margarine
1 tsp. dried mint

Cook peas according to package directions. Sauté mushrooms in the butter or margarine. When peas are tender, drain, add mushrooms, juices and the finely crushed mint leaves. Serves 4.

Fresh or canned peas may also be used. One pound of fresh peas in pod yields 1 cup of hulled peas.

Mint tea is served often as a refreshing drink and a gesture of friendship by the people from Morocco through Turkey. It is prepared before the guests in beautiful brass or silver pots. Either black or green tea is used. The sugar is added to the brewing. The following recipe makes 4 cups of tea.

MINT TEA

4-5 tsp. tea leaves
8-10 sprigs of mint
½ cup sugar

Rinse the pot with boiling water to heat it. Put the tea, mint sprigs and sugar in the pot and add 4 cups of boiling water. Let steep for 7-10 minutes. Serves 4.

ROMAN APPLES

6 baking apples
1 cup sugar
¼ cup (½ stick) butter or margarine
½ tsp. cinnamon
20 fresh mint leaves or 1 tsp. crushed dried mint

Wash, core and peel upper fourth of each apple. Place in a casserole. Fill cavities with sugar. Put a pat of butter on each apple. Sprinkle with cinnamon and finely crushed mint. Bake at 375 degrees until tender—about 40 minutes. Baste occasionally with the syrup.

mustard

Jesus' parables using a mustard seed are some of the best known of all. His references to its small size are well founded. ". . . a grain of mustard seed. . . . is less than all the seeds. . . ." (Mark 4:31) Black mustard seeds count out to about 12,740 per ounce, 203,840 per pound.

The mustard plant was used in Bible times and before for both its seeds and its greens just as we do today. The seeds were prepared as a condiment as well as pressed for their oil. Archaeological evidence indicates that mustard has been known to man since prehistoric times. The Sumerians who achieved a high civilization in the Tigris-Euphrates valley in the third and fourth millenia B.C. raised mustard.

Black mustard to which Jesus referred is mixed with white mustard, salt, vinegar and spices to make our familiar hot dog spread. Despite its familiarity to us in this form we use mustard far less than it was in ancient times. The name itself is a corruption of "must-seeds" since the seeds were processed in Roman days by saturating them in "must" the word for unfermented grape juice. Romans used the seeds extensively in medicine. Perhaps some of our readers will remember from childhood the mustard-poultices used to treat chest colds.

If you buy the whole seeds you will find they have practically no odor. Only when they are crushed in the presence of a little water do they give off their sharp, piercing scent. One of the more interesting recipes in our collection is from Columella, a Latin writer in the first century A.D. For table use he recommended crushed seeds prepared with vinegar and mixed with pine kernels and almonds.

In Shakespeare's time many people put mustard on their pancakes just as today some people put mustard on apple pie. Probably there are very few homes in the U.S. without prepared mustard on hand. But most of it is quite bland. The French, on the other hand, mix their mustard with herbs of various kinds so it has quite a different taste from ours.

If you'd like to give a fillip to that prepared mustard you have on hand try these ideas. For every 2 tbs. of prepared mustard add 1 tsp. of curry powder or chili powder. The former is excellent on egg sandwiches or in potato salad and the latter on hot dogs, hamburgers and cold cuts. Other herbs you can mix with mustard are basil, horseradish, lovage, marjoram, oregano, rosemary, sage, tarragon, parsley and thyme. Try 'em a bit at a time until you find the ones you like best. When mixing with a dry herb it is best to let it marinate over night.

Mustard has been used as a sauce for thousands of years. A recipe from the time of Christ for mustard sauce on boar, sausages and other meats calls for mustard with oil, vinegar, pepper, lovage, cumin, asafoetida, oregano, pine kernels, dates, honey and liquamen, which was a salty concoction. Here's our modern adaptation. It is surprisingly good on roast pork or ham.

SWEET MUSTARD SAUCE

- 1 tsp. salt
- ½ tsp. pepper
- 2 ribs celery with leaves, chopped
- 1 tsp. cumin
- 1 tsp. oregano
- 2 cups water
- ½ cup dates, cut up
- ¼ cup honey
- 2 tbs. prepared mustard
- ¼ tsp. Worcestershire sauce

Put salt, pepper, celery, cumin and oregano to boil in the water. Simmer 20 minutes. Let stand to cool. Strain. Add remaining ingredients. Simmer 5 minutes. If you wish to thicken use a paste of cornstarch. Serve hot over sliced roast pork or ham or on the side.

MUSTARD SAUCE #2

- 3 tbs. butter or margarine
- 2 tbs. flour
- 1 tsp. prepared mustard
- 1 cup boiling stock (or 1 cup water with 2 beef bouillon cubes dissolved)

Melt butter. Blend in flour. Add mustard and boiling stock. Stir and serve. Great with corned beef, fish and other meats.

MUSTARD HAM SAUCE

½ cup currant jelly
½ cup prepared mustard

Heat jelly over low fire until it melts. Stir in mustard and pour in a small mold. Refrigerate until ready to use.

MUSTARD GREENS

2 lb. mustard greens
6 to 8 slices bacon, sautéed and crumbled
¼ cup lemon juice
salt and pepper

Wash the greens carefully in several waters. Cut off and discard coarse stems. Cut crosswise into 1 inch slices. Put in a kettle with ½ inch of water and 1 tsp. salt. Boil until tender, about 8 to 10 minutes. Drain. Add lemon juice to sautéed bacon, heat and pour over greens. Toss lightly and serve hot. Serves 4.

OLIVE OIL

Olive oil being extracted from crushed olives by pressure.

"Oil and perfume make the heart glad," Proverbs 27:9 (RSV) tells us. As food, medicine, ointment and fuel for their lamps, olive oil was essential to the people of Bible times.

Over 5,000 years ago oil was being extracted from olives in Palestine. In the centuries that followed, olive presses became a common sight from Crete to Egypt. Sinhue, the Egyptian exile who lived in northern Palestine about 1960 B.C., wrote of abundant olive trees. Actual remains of olive oil have been found in jugs over 4,000 years old in a tomb on the island of Naxos in the Aegean Sea. Before 2000 B.C. the Egyptians imported olive oil from Crete, Syria and Palestine so it was obviously an important item of commerce and wealth.

In the hot Mediterranean lands olive oil was a blessing as an ointment applied as we do suntan lotions today. Isaiah 1:6 (RSV) indicates that olive oil was used to soften wounds much as we turn to salves. But it was for food, of course, that olive oil was used in greatest abundance, as a spread on bread and fat for cooking. Time after time in Exodus and Leviticus the Lord calls for olive oil in burnt offerings or as an anointing oil as well as mixed with fine flour or put on unleavened wafers.

One of the most touching stories about olive oil is that of the widow who fed Elijah with oil and meal from her scanty supply. For this she was blessed by a miracle. From that time on "The jar of meal was not spent, neither did the cruse of oil fail. . . ." (I Kings 17:16 RSV)

Olive oil has taken on almost a sacred meaning to Christians because it is so closely associated with the garden of Gethsemane where Jesus was betrayed and arrested. Gethsemane means literally "oil press." It lies at the bottom of the Mount of Olives which was covered with olive trees in Bible days. The olive presses at Gethsemane must have been one of Jesus' last memories of that garden where he had gone to pray.

To this day in Crete they prepare olive oil in the ancient manner. The olives are covered with hot water and then crushed. They are held in large vats with a drain at the bottom. The oil floats to the surface. When the process is complete the water is drained from the bottom and only the pure oil is left at the top.

The Roman, Cato (234 to 149 B.C.) gives careful attention to the making of olive oil. He recommended ripe olives which yielded a "green oil."

For the Greeks olive oil served a myriad uses. Athletes as well as others massaged it into their bodies before exercising. It was important as a preservative for fabrics. When Alexander was in the capital of Persia, Susa, in 331 B.C. he was shown fabrics kept in this manner. The preservative was a mixture of honey and olive oil.

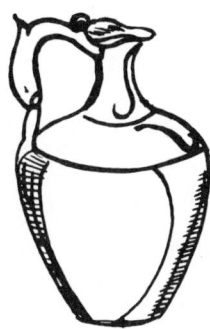

Of course, cooking still remains the most important use. Roman chef Apicius called for olive oil in so many recipes it would take pages even to list them. Like all oils, that of the olive is high in calories. One tablespoon of corn, cottonseed, soybean or olive oil contains 125 calories. Vitamins and minerals are lacking. Obviously, oils are 100% fat. But there is a difference in the nature of the fat. Some are higher in saturated fats. Others come off better with the unsaturated fats, oleic and linoleic.

Nutritionists and scientific investigators into heart disease have brought public attention to the importance in our diet of saturated versus unsaturated fatty acids. So, it is interesting to compare olive oil with some of the others. Most fats contains both types. But solid fats, like butter and lard or any fat from meat, are primarily saturated. On the other hand, fats from vegetable sources, like those in the table below, and fats from fish contain a higher percentage of unsaturated fats.

GRAMS OF FATTY ACIDS PER 100 GRAMS OF OIL
(In descending order saturated fat)

	Saturated Fatty Acids	Unsaturated Oleic	Fatty Acids Linoleic
Butter	46 grams	27 grams	2 grams
Cottonseed	25	21	50
Peanut	18	47	29
Soybean	15	20	52
Sesame	14	38	42
Olive	11	76	7
Corn	10	28	53
Safflower	8	15	72

The United States still imports considerable olive oil although there is production from California grown olives which were introduced by the Spaniards to the first missions there.

Today the finest or "virgin" olive oil is made from fruit gathered before it is fully ripe. It is peeled and gently pressed without heat. Olive oil used for food may be a clear white, golden yellow or yellowish green. But it is all good eating. When heated, olive oil has a low smoking point compared with most of the vegetable oils and hydrogenated shortenings. In this sense it is much like butter. It's also like butter in that after a can or jar is once opened it should be refrigerated to prevent rancidity.

Use it as a direct substitute for butter in cooking as well as for a salad oil. We always put a tablespoon in with our dry spaghetti when cooking it to prevent sticking. And we often serve the following dressing on our salads.

SALAD DRESSING

 8 oz. (1 cup) olive oil
 2 lemons, juiced
  tarragon vinegar added to
  lemon juice to make ¾ cup
 ½ tsp. Tabasco
 1 tsp. Worcestershire sauce
 ½ tsp. salt
  cracked pepper to taste
 3 garlic cloves, crushed

Combine ingredients and shake well. Let stand at room temperature to blend for about an hour. Then refrigerate and use as needed. Makes almost 2 cups.

Corinthian oil flask

salt

In an ancient salt pan slaves crack out the pieces after sea water has dried and caked.

Salt is so insignificant in price and so readily available it is difficult to realize something so seemingly minor has caused men to be sold into slavery, empires to rise and decline, crime to increase and men to become sworn brothers.

Far-fetched, extreme statements? Not at all! In 1708 a French churchman told of peasants thrown into prison when they sought merely to get salt for their families who were sick for lack of it. By controlling the armies who guarded salt sources, rulers in the ancient world literally had life and death power over their people. As recently as 1882 a traveler in East Africa was offered a slave for four loaves of salt. In fact, salt is so essential to life that civilizations have flourished only where it is readily available.

In Bible lands where salt was plentiful it was still a precious commodity used to preserve meat and fish and other edibles. The Lord himself commanded that *all* meat offerings should be seasoned with salt. (Leviticus 2:13) In this same passage is the phrase "salt of the covenant" which refers to the belief that when one person ate another man's salt he came under that man's protection. For the people of Bible times salt was the symbol of hospitality. If men ate bread *and* salt together they created thereby an unbreakable vow of friendship. When Jesus told his disciples how important their mission was he said: "Ye are the salt of the earth. . . ." (Matthew 5:13) To eat the salt of the king was to owe him undying fealty.

A Sumerian proverb from some time prior to 2000 B.C. reads: "When a poor man has died, do not try to revive him! When he had bread he had no salt; when he had salt he had no bread." For these people salt was an important item in the temple storehouses. It preserved their fish, flavored their food and cured their ills.

In Bible times the Dead Sea was called the Salt Sea and with good reason. It is the saltiest body of water in the world with a 30% concentration of salt versus about 3% for ocean water. Jericho, one of the world's oldest villages, is at the north end of the Dead Sea. There is no doubt some of its inhabitants of long ago worked the "solar pans" around the edges of this sea. These are shallow rectangular areas on the ground surrounded by low dikes.

The salty water is let into them and permitted to evaporate until the salt is ready to scoop out. This method of making salt is at least 5,000 years old yet 40% of the salt produced today is still made the same way.

Our body requires that the salt concentration in the blood be constant. If the level falls, certain hormones reduce salt lost through excretion and perspiration. However, if no salt whatsoever is taken in and some losses—that cannot be stopped—continue through the kidneys and perspiration our body faces a dilemma. It proceeds to draw off and excrete water to keep the proper salt concentration in the blood. If the process continues the body becomes drier and drier even to the point of death.

Conversely, if insufficient water is the problem our body mechanism works in reverse. It attempts to retain all possible water. But through the uncontrollable loss of some water through evaporation the salt concentration in the blood rises to the point where this too can lead to death.

In areas of the world where meat and fish provide a large part of the diet there is enough salt in such foods to create no problem. On the other hand, if the diet is primarily vegetarian our body needs two to five grams of salt per day which must be supplied by pure salt. Interestingly, salt is habit forming. People who are accustomed to a lot of it get to the point of wanting more than their body requires.

The part salt has played in the history of man can fill a book. To give you recipes is superfluous. But you may find the following suggestions helpful.

If you're fishing, here's a secret to keep your catch fresh for 24 hours without ice. Bleed and clean fish. Prepare mixture of one cup regular table salt to 1 tbs. pepper. Rub well into fish. Put fish in a container and pack green leaves around it. Cover with several layers of sacking or paper. Keep latter moist but don't let it touch the fish directly. When you're ready to cook, rinse well and handle just as you would fresh fish.

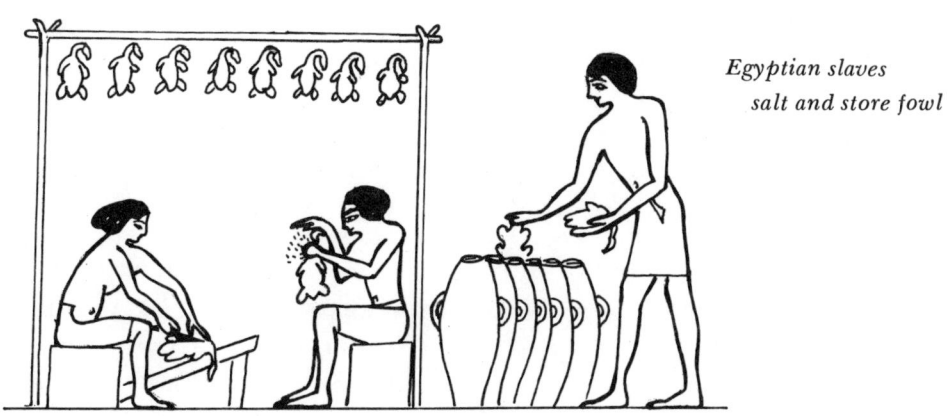

Egyptian slaves salt and store fowl

Want to keep your cake icing from sugaring? Add a pinch of salt. If you whip cream or egg whites a sprinkle of salt will help the process. To keep lumps out of your gravy add salt to the flour you use for thickening. Many people add a pinch of salt to their coffee when brewing. It takes out the bitterness even if the coffee is too strong. Same for tea which salt makes smoother. In cocoa salt makes the flavor a bit richer.

When boiling eggs add a teaspoon of salt to the water and a cracked shell will not break further. If you're not sure whether an egg is fresh you can test it in a mixture of 8 ounces of water with 1 teaspoon of salt. If the egg sinks it is fresh. If it floats it has begun to "turn."

Seasoned salts are popular. They are a mix of spices, herbs and salt designed as all-purpose seasoning. Many restaurants put them on the table with the regular salt and pepper. Once you get used to them you'll find yourself shaking a bit in everything from meats and vegetables to sauces and dairy foods.

Let's not forget iodized salt. In 1921 scientific experiments established that iodine added to the diet of children in locations where it was not present in the soil (and therefore the food) could prevent the development of goiter. There are a number of such areas in the U.S. The largest one is around the Great Lakes.

Most people do not realize that the only spots in the U.S. where the soil and the food grown on it contain sufficient iodine are a narrow strip along the Atlantic coast and the Gulf of Mexico plus a few, isolated locales in the central western states. The only reliable, natural source of iodine is ocean fish and sea foods. But it's simple and safe to get your iodine from iodized salt. Goiter has disappeared in countries like Switzerland and Austria where *only* iodized salt is sold.

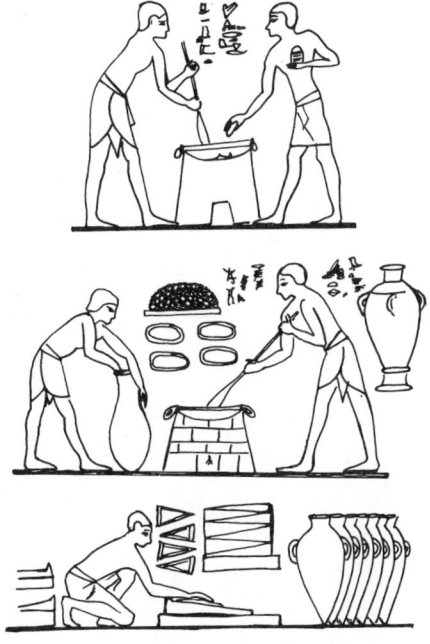

In 3500 B.C. this painting depicted Egyptian candymakers. At top they make dough, middle scene shows them mixing it with honey or dates and at bottom it is being cut into triangles.

SUGARCANE

If one were to look at a Concordance to the Bible it might be difficult to trace references to sugarcane. The only obvious one is that of Isaiah 43:24 "Thou hast brought me no sweet cane...."

But a look at the original Hebrew word for sugarcane and the places it appears in the Bible throws a good deal more light on our most popular sweetener. The Hebrew word is "keneh," or "kaneh." In Exodus 30:23 (King James Version) the original for sweet calamus is "keneh bosem." It means "spiced or sweet cane." This same word has been translated "calamus" in Ezekiel 27:19 "... bright iron, cassia and *calamus* were in thy market." Although scholars may quarrel over the precise translation of "keneh" as it appears in various places there is no doubt the sweet cane of the Bible is our sugarcane.

We know that sugarcane was growing in New Guinea as early as 8000 B.C. and at a very early date spread from this little island off the north coast of Australia to China and India. As early as 2800 B.C. we have evidence there was trade between sugar-growing India and Mesopotamia. Whether sugar was traded at that time has not been established. But there was also a brisk merchant ship business between India and Arabia which ultimately deposited all types of Indian commodities in the entire Near East via Egypt and overland Arabian routes.

Putting all the evidence together—the trade with India and the presence of sugar there—we have no doubt the people of Bible days were quite familiar with sugarcane. By the time written records are plentiful on the subject of sugar we find it well established. The Greek geographer Strabo described a honey that was extracted from canes or reeds. Another Greek, Dioscorides, who lived in the first century A.D., wrote that in India there is a sort of hardened honey called sugar. He noted that it was found on canes in India and is hard as salt and brittle under the teeth. Sugar is mentioned in the Sama Veda, sacred writings of India that date to about 1500 B.C.

Of course the people of Bible times chewed the sweet cane itself as a candy. But they were also adept at squeezing oil from many seeds and plants so it is logical to assume they squeezed the juice from the cane. If they did and let it evaporate a little in that hot climate they would have had a product quite similar to molasses. In modern sugar mills molasses is the liquid that is separated from sugar when the first crystallization takes place. At this point the crystallized sucrose is called raw or brown sugar. It is a source of a variety of minerals. For instance, brown sugar has more calcium, phosphorus, sodium and potassium than honey. Its iron content is half again that of our popular iron source, cooked spinach.

But the beautifully refined product we all prefer is, of course, white sugar. The refining process removes most of the components of the raw sugar, including the color, to leave a remarkably pure carbohydrate called sucrose. The human body converts this to energy with exceptional speed.

Today our fiftieth state, Hawaii, produces more than one-fourth of U.S. sugar supplies although sugarcane is grown also in southern states like Louisiana. Practically all sugar used in the western two-thirds of the U.S. comes from domestic sources. That used in the east is imported for the most part.

Since sugar is so widely used in making cakes, candies, pies and puddings we thought you might like a very ancient and delightfully different Persian recipe.

FLOWER PETAL PRESERVES

1 lb. fresh rose petals or ⅓ lb. dried
   (Any highly fragrant blossom or petal will do like quince, violet, orange and jasmine)
1 lb. (2 cups) sugar
1 cup hot water
½ tsp. cardamom, crushed
½ cup almonds, crushed

Wash fresh blossoms gently in cold water. If dried petals are used let them stand in cold water one hour. Drain and cover with fresh water and bring to slow boil. Boil 2 minutes. Drain. Rinse in ice water. Drain again. Boil sugar and water until it spins a long thread. Add cardamom and nuts. Boil 5 minutes more. Add petals and return to a boil for 1 minute. Remove from heat and pour into small preserve jars. Cool. Cover tightly and keep in a cool place.

Since molasses might have been the most ancient form of sugar as we know it here is a recipe for a molasses cake. Try baking it in a 10 by 15 inch sheet cake tin. Then cut it in bars. Or you can bake it in a smaller but deeper tin, if you prefer. Just give it a few minutes extra time in the oven. Anyway you bake it you'll find it very tasty and filled with enough nourishing foods that you won't worry if the children eat it for breakfast.

MOLASSES CAKE

½ cup sugar
¼ cup butter
1 cup molasses
2 eggs
½ cup milk
2 cups flour, sifted before measuring
1 tsp. baking powder
1 tsp. cinnamon
½ tsp. salt
¼ tsp. soda
¼ tsp. ground cloves
1 cup (4¾ oz. package) walnut pieces
1 cup dates, cut up

Cream sugar and butter together. Add molasses and eggs. Beat until smooth. Resift flour with baking powder, cinnamon, salt, soda and cloves and add alternately with milk. Stir in walnuts and dates and spread batter in a 10″ x 15″ sheet cake tin. Bake at 375° for 15 minutes, or until a toothpick inserted in the center comes out clean.

VINEGAR

From the 7th century B.C. a Corinthian wine jug.

Vinegar means literally "sour wine" from the French "vin" i.e. wine plus "aigre," sour. Wine turns to vinegar when its alcohol is completely converted by yeasts into acetic acid.

Consequently vinegar is probably as old as wine which in turn is old as recorded history. Any sweet liquid will turn to an alcoholic beverage by the action of natural yeasts. If it remains exposed to the air a different kind of yeast turns it to vinegar. As a result there are many kinds of vinegar from such sources as cider, pears, peaches, plum, figs, oranges, pineapples, berries, etc.

In Numbers 6:3 there is reference to "wine vinegar." In Ruth 2:14 of the King James version of the Bible Ruth is told to dip her food in vinegar. And in Proverbs 10:26 the astringent action of vinegar is aptly described: "As vinegar to the teeth and as smoke to the eyes." Just before Jesus died on the cross he was given a sponge soaked in vinegar. (Mark 15:36) Most Bible interpreters believe this was actually the sour wine of the common soldier which is much like vinegar.

By Roman times gourmets demanded certain types of vinegar. The Roman Horace described a banquet in which a variety of delicacies were served including the vinegar from Lesbos. Cato, another Roman who lived in the second century B.C., gives directions for preserving lentils and green olives in vinegar. He extolled the health virtues of cabbage and particularly recommended it be served raw, dipped in vinegar or chopped, dried and seasoned with salt and vinegar. The great Roman chef Apicius called for vinegar in practically all of his sauces as well as for preserving fish, oysters and turnips.

During Prohibition days almost no wine vinegar was made in the U.S. but today it has come into its own again. French and other foreign cooks have continued to demand wine vinegar in their cookery for it imparts a taste of its own that is lacking in distilled white vinegars. Nonetheless the largest volume of vinegar in the U.S. is either distilled or made from apple cider. Of course, all vinegars contain the same essential ingredient, acetic acid. But the juice from which a vinegar is made and the herbs and other flavorings added to it make for a wide variety.

A best selling book of recent years was Dr. D. C. Jarvis "Folk Medicine" in which he vigorously recommended the use of apple cider vinegar practically as a medicine.

Certainly the ancients ascribed medicinal qualities to it. But health food or not vinegar is an essential item in every home. It is called for in so many recipes we have decided to give you some uncommon ones. You'll find the pie quite reminiscent of mincemeat but better.

VINEGAR PIE

1/3 cup mild vinegar
1¾ cups sugar
1 cup raisins, chopped
1 package (5½ oz.) walnut meats, chopped (about 1 cup)
1 tsp. vanilla
3 tbs. butter, melted
2 tbs. water
1 tsp. allspice
¼ tsp. salt
4 eggs, beaten

1 unbaked pie shell, 9 inch

Combine all the ingredients, folding the eggs in last. Fill the pie shell. Bake at 375 degrees until filling sets and crust is lightly browned, about 35 to 40 minutes. May be topped with whipped cream. Serves 6 to 8. Delicious hot or cold.

POT ROAST VINAIGRETTE

3 pound beef pot roast
1 cup mild vinegar
1 cup water
1 medium size onion, sliced
2 or 3 bay leaves
¼ cup brown sugar
1 tsp. whole peppercorns
1 clove garlic
salt and pepper to taste

Salt and pepper meat. Place in glass bowl. In spice bag made of thin muslin or cheesecloth place bay leaves, peppercorns and garlic loosely. Tie shut. Put in sauce pan with remaining ingredients. Heat just to a boil. Pour over meat. Let stand overnight. Turn meat occasionally. When ready to cook, drain and dry meat but save liquid. Sear in heavy pan until well browned on both sides. Add cupful of liquid, cover and place in 325 degree oven. Roast 2 to 3 hours until quite tender, adding liquid as needed. Thicken gravy with flour (2 tbs. stirred to smooth paste in 2 to 3 tbs. water).

If you have never introduced children to the fun and laughter that goes with pulling taffy, don't wait another day. This easy recipe is one they can manage quite well with little supervision. But if they haven't actually pulled candy they may need some direction with that part.

VINEGAR TAFFY

2 tbs. butter or margarine
2 cups sugar
½ cup cider vinegar

Melt the butter in a good sized saucepan. Add sugar and vinegar and bring to a boil. Stir until the sugar is dissolved, then occasionally until it forms a brittle ball in cold water. Pour on a buttered plate to cool.

With lightly buttered fingers gather the candy up. Stretch and fold it until it becomes quite firm and has a pale satin sheen. Stretch it out and snip off 1 inch pieces, letting them drop onto a plate or waxed paper.

If pulling taffy is a little more than you care to get involved in, here's another vinegar candy. This one has the sweet-sour taste reminiscent of "sour balls" of years ago.

CANDY VINAIGRETTE

2 tbs. butter or margarine
2 cups brown sugar, firmly packed
½ cup vinegar

Melt butter and add sugar and vinegar. Boil gently until it makes a firm ball in cold water. Remove from heat and beat until it starts to thicken. Pour out on a buttered plate to cool.

WINE

At Thebes in Egypt in the tomb of Nakht is this wall painting. Slaves pick grapes at right while those at the left tread out the juice. 15th century B.C.

One of the more controversial subjects in the Bible is wine. Some commentators have suggested that the wine of the Bible was grape juice unfermented and, therefore, non-alcoholic. However, this possibility is negated by the very first mention of wine in the Bible, the story of Noah's drunkenness. (Genesis 9:21)

It was this kind of overdoing the Bible constantly warns about. A representative admonition is Ephesians 5:18. "And be not drunk with wine, wherein is excess...." On the other hand wine appears as an offering to the Lord. "And for a drink offering thou shalt offer the third part of a hin of wine, for a sweet savor unto the Lord." (Numbers 15:7) Wine is considered a gift from God in passages like Isaiah 25:6. "And in the mountain shall the

Lord of hosts make unto all people a feast of fat things: a feast of wines on the lees...."

In the ancient ruins of Lachish, 30 miles southwest of Jerusalem, archaeologists have found evidence of wine making. The time was the early Bronze Age about 3000 B.C. which was a thousand years before Abraham. Urukagina, a king of Sumeria, mentions royal wine cellars in 2379 B.C. Sinuhe, an Egyptian exile in northern Palestine in 1960 B.C., remarked that the country had more wine than water. Since wine goes so far back into mankind's history it is no surprise the ancient records abound with all types: white wine, spiced, sweet, sharp, myrtle, violet rose, etc.

The grape is native to Turkey and the Lebanon mountains that extend from Syria to Israel. From this variety of vine, vitis vinifera, come most of California's wine-making grapes. Eastern U.S. grapes are generally domesticated varieties of native American species.

WINE CUSTARD

4 eggs
4 tbs. sugar
4 tbs. cream sherry

Break the eggs into the top of a double boiler. Beat them until they are light and frothy. Continue beating while you add the sugar slowly, 1 tbs. at a time. Add wine. Place over boiling water and continue beating until it reaches a custard-like consistency. Spoon into sherbet or champagne glasses. May be served warm or chilled. Serves 4.

If you find this a little too strong in flavor, use 3 tbs. of wine with 1 tbs. of water.

A scene showing Egyptians drawing off wine from the lees, then mixing it.

The next time you celebrate some festive occasion you might enjoy serving guests a wine punch that could easily have been drunk 2,000 or more years ago. All the ingredients are old as history. The pomegranate juice called for is known today as grenadine. It is as ancient a fruit as the grape and was used itself to make wine as told in Songs of Solomon 8:2. "I would cause thee to drink of spiced wine of the juice of my pomegranate."

SPICY ROMAN PUNCH

1 large bottle (Fifth) dry white dinner wine like Rhine or Riesling
1½ tbs. fresh cinnamon sticks
1 tbs. fresh or dried mint leaves
½ tsp. fresh anise seeds
4 oz. grenadine syrup

Chill wine 4 hours. Meanwhile crush or chop fine the mint, cinnamon and anise. Mix with 3 tbs. water and grenadine. Cook over low heat 10 minutes. Stir frequently. Let stand 1 to 4 hours. When ready pour wine into mixture. Stir until syrup dissolves. Strain. Pour into iced punch bowl. For garnish float on top white grapes, 2 cinnamon sticks and, if you can find one, the scooped out seeds from fresh pomegranate.

If you've never had a Wassail Bowl during the holidays now's the time to plan one. The name comes from Old Norse meaning "be in good health." In Olde England the wassail bowl was present at any festive occasion especially the cold holidays. It was concocted of ale or wine flavored with spices and ingredients like sugar, toast, roast apples, raisins, etc. Here's one adapted from a California Wine Advisory Board recipe.

HOT WINE WASSAIL BOWL

- 6 apples
- 2 bottles (Fifths) Tokay, Sherry or Muscatel wine
- ½ tsp. nutmeg
- ½ tsp. cinnamon
- 3 cloves
- ½ cup sugar
- 1 tbs. grated lemon rind
- 4 eggs
- 1 cup blanched almonds (optional)

Bake apples as follows: Core. Peel a strip one inch wide around top edge. Fill center with sugar. Place in deep baking pan. Pour 1 cup water around apples. Bake uncovered at 375 degrees about 45 minutes or until tender when stuck with fork. Baste at least 4 times. Meanwhile in double boiler heat the wine but do not boil. Add nutmeg, cinnamon, cloves, sugar, lemon rind. Separate egg yolks and beat whites until stiff. Beat egg yolks. Fold in whites. Add hot wine slowly. Beat until frothy. Put baked apples and almonds in bowl. Pour hot wine mix over them. Serve in warmed mugs. Yield: ten 5 oz. servings.

Index

a

ALMONDS	99
Aaron's Almond Fudge	101
Almond and Tuna Casserole	102
Almond Butter	161
Heavenly Tea Cakes	101
ANISE (see Dill)	203
Finocchio Florentine	205
Aphrodite's Salad	214
Apicius' Appetizer, Brains	18
APPLES	51
Apple Casserole	54
Apples in Robes	53
Eden Fall Salad	54
Roman Apples, Mint	218
APRICOTS	55
Apricots Abigail, a fritter	57
Glazed Apricots	58
King Solomon's Gold, gelatine	57
Spicy Apricots	58
ARTICHOKES	127
Athenian Artichokes	129
Crown of Cardoon	131
Fresh Whole Artichokes	130

B

BARLEY	103
Barzillai, soup	106
Iberian Barley	106
Poor Lad's Loaf, bread	111
Ruth's Casserole	105
BAY LEAVES	187
Broiled Kidneys	31
Marinade for Budget Steak	189
Rebecca's Tasty Dish	190
Shrimp Espanol	189
BEANS	132
Four Bean Salad	135
Green Beans Ezekiel	134
Green Beans with Apple Jelly	135
Bedouin Bread	110
Beef and Veal	
Aegean Island Stew	194
Apicius' Appetizer	18

Baked Brains with Egg	18
Beef Yoganoff	183
Brains, Fried	17
Brains with Scrambled Eggs	17
Cabbage Rolls with Raisins	90
Corn 'n Olives	82
Dolmas	150
Hamburgers with Cumin	202
Liver with Garlic Sauce	40
Liver Vinaigrette	40
Pot Roast Vinaigrette	241
Ruth's Casserole	105
Spaghetti Sauce Comino	201
Sultan's Soup	87
Veal Kidney Chops	30
Wheat Meat Loaf	123
Beef Yoganoff	183
Belgian Endive	147
Blintz, Cottage Cheese	171
BRAINS	15
Apicius' Appetizer	18
Baked with Eggs	18
Fried Brains	17
To Prepare	17
With Scrambled Eggs	17
BREAD	107
Bedouin Bread	110
Poor Lad's Loaf, Barley	111
Bulgur, How to Cook	122
BUTTER	159
Almond Butter	161
Butter Balls	162
Butter Horn Pastries	163
Herb Butter	161
Maitre d' Hotel	161

C

Cabbage Rolls with Raisins	90
Cakes	
Cretan Cake, Raisins	91
Date Cake	66
Molasses Cake	237
St. John's Cake, Carob	62
Yogurt-Lemon Cake	184
Candy	
Aaron's Almond Fudge	101
Candy Vinaigrette	242
Caravan Candy	70
Cleopatra's Kisses	214
Crazy Candy	96
Tadmor Delight	66
Vinegar Taffy	242
Cantaloupe	
Melon Cup	77
Persian Pie	78
CAROB	59
Cake, St. John's	62
Icing, uncooked	62
Syrup	61
Casseroles	
Almond-Tuna	102
Apple	54
Corn 'n Olives	82
Lamb Skillet Pie	36
Ruth's Casserole, Barley	105
Tuna-Noodle	48

CASSIA (see Cinnamon)	191
CHEESE	164
Cheese Custard Pie	167
Cheese Rounds	166
Cheese Sauce	179
Fondeau	167
Chicken	
Damascus, Coriander	198
Paté, Livers	39
Romano, Cumin	202
Walnut Chicken	119
Christmas Pudding	69
CINNAMON, CASSIA	191
Aegean Island Stew	194
Cinnamon Suggestions	194
Solomon's Cantaloupe	193
Cleopatra's Kisses	214
Cookies	
Date Bars	66
Heavenly Tea Cakes	101
CORIANDER	195
Damascus Chicken	198
Fish of Galilee	21
Pork Mediterranee	198
Seraphim Pudding	197
Corn 'n Olives	82
COTTAGE CHEESE	168
Curried	170
Delilah's Dessert	170
Elah Cheese Rolls, Blintz	171
Cretan Cake	91
CUCUMBERS	136
Cream of Cucumber Soup	139
Cucumbers 'n Laban	138
Tiberian Cucumbers	139
CUMIN	199
Chicken Romano	202
Hamburgers with Cumin	202
Spaghetti Sauce Comino	201
Custard, Wine	244

D

Damascus Chicken	198
DANDELION GREENS	140
Boiled	143
Coat of Jacob Salad	143
DATES	63
Cake	66
Tadmor Delight	66
Tamarah Pie	65
Delilah's Dessert	170
DILL, ANISE and FENNEL	203
Fennel Roma	206
Finocchio Florentine	205
Persian Rice	205
Dolmas	150
Drawn Butter	160
Dressing, Goose	26

E

Eden Fall Salad	54
EGGS	172
Baked with Brains	18
Creamed	174
Egg Sauce	179
Roman Hors d' Oeuvres	175
Scrambled with Brains	17
Venecia	175
Elah Cheese Rolls	171
ENDIVE	144
Baked Belgian Endive	147
Egyptian Style	146
Salad	146
Eshcol Surprise, Salad	74

F

FENNEL (see Dill)	203
Fennel Roma	206
FIGS	67
Caravan Candy	70
Christmas Pudding	69
Festive Figs	68
Finocchio Florentine	205
FISH (also see Seafood)	19
Baked Fish	22
Fish de Medici	213
Fish of Galilee	21
Simon Peter Fish Stew	23
Sole Veronique	73
Flower Petal Preserves	236
Fowl	
Chicken Romano	202
Chicken with Walnuts	119
Damascus Chicken	198
Goose, Roast	25
Patrician Paté, Livers	39
Sinuhe Salad	27
Fried Brains	17
Fudge, Aaron's Almond	101

G

GARLIC	207
Ghee	160
GOOSE	24
Dressing for	26
Liver Hors d' Oeuvres	27
Roast Goose	25
Sinuhe Salad	27
GRAPE LEAVES	148
Cocktail Dolmas	151
Dolmas	150
GRAPES	71
Eshcol Surprise	74
Frost on the Grapes	73
Sole Veronique	73
Vine and Sea Salad	74
GREEN BEANS	132
Four Bean Salad	135
Green Beans Ezekiel	134
With Apple Jelly	135
GREEN ONIONS	152
Boiled on Toast	154
Fried	155
Leek Soup	156

h

Ham
  Baked Endive with
    Ham   147
  Lehi Lentils   115
Heavenly Tea Cakes   101
Herb Butter   161
HONEY   211
  Aphrodite's Salad
    Dressing   214
  Cleopatra's Kisses   214
  Fish de Medici   213
Hors d'Oeuvres
  Artichoke, Crown of
    Cardoon   131
  Brains, Apicius
    Appetizer   18
  Cheese Rounds   166
  Eggs, Roman   175
  Goose Liver   27
  Grape Leaves, Dolmas   151
  Liver Paté   39

i

Iberian Barley   106

k

KIDNEYS   28
  Broiled with Garlic   31
  Kingly Kidneys   30
  Veal Kidney Chops   30
King Solomon's Gold,
  Apricots   57
King Solomon's Nut Loaf   118

l

LAMB   32
  Lamb Skillet Pie   36
  Mint Sauce for Lamb   217
  Passover Lamb   35
  Rebecca's Tasty Dish   190
  Roast Leg of Lamb   34
  Sultan's Soup   87
Leek Soup   156
Lehi Lentils   115
LENTILS   112
  Lentils Esau   114
  Lehi Lentils, Soup   115
  Lentils with Greens   115
LIVER   37
  Broiled with Garlic   40
  Goose Liver   27
  Patrician Paté   39
  Vinaigrette   40

m

Maitre d'Hotel Butter	161
Marinade for Budget Steak	189
MILK	176
Cheese Sauce	179
Egg Sauce	179
Onion Sauce	179
Roman Custard	178
White Sauce	179
MINT	215
Mint Tea	218
Mintho's Peas	217
Roman Apples	218
Sauce for Lamb	217
Molasses Cake	237
MUSKMELONS	75
Miriam's Melon Cup	77
Persian Pie	78
MUSTARD	219
Mustard Greens	222
Mustard Ham Sauce	222
Mustard Sauce	221
Sweet Mustard Sauce	221

n

Nuts	
Almonds	99
Walnuts	116
Nut Loaf	118

o

OLIVE OIL	223
Salad Dressing	227
OLIVES	79
Olives with Corn	82
Salad of Sheba	81
Sauce Italiano	81
Onion and Apple Casserole	54
Onions, Boiled on Toast	154
Onions, Fried	155
Onion Sauce	179

p

Passover Lamb	35
Paté, Liver	39
Persian Rice	205
Pharaoh's Fruit Bowl	95
Pies	
Cheese Custard	167
Persian Pie, Muskmelon	78
Tamarah Pie, Dates	65
Vinegar Pie	240
Pilaf	122
POMEGRANATES	83
Sultan's Soup	87
Poor Lad's Loaf	111
Pork Mediterranee	198
Puddings	
Christmas Pudding	69
Seraphim Pudding	197

R

RABBIT	41
Fricassee	44
Oven Fried	44
Rabbit in Wine Sauce	43
RAISINS	88
Cabbage Rolls	90
Cider Sauce for Ham	92
Cretan Cake	91
Rebecca's Tasty Dish	190
Rice, Persian	205
Rice Pilaf	122
Roman Custard	178
Roman Hors d'Oeuvres	175
Ruth's Casserole	105

S

St. John's Cake	62
Salads	
Apple, Eden Fall	54
Artichoke, Crown of Cardoon	131
Bean, Four Bean	135
Cucumber-Tuna	48
Dandelion, Coat of Jacob	143
Endive	146
Fruit, Aphrodite's	214
Grape, Eshcol Surprise	74
Grape, Vine and Sea	74
Goose, Sinuhe	27
Melon, Miriam's	77
Melon, Pharaoh's Fruit Bowl	95
Olive, Salad of Sheba	81
Shrimp, Vine and Sea	74
Tuna-Cucumber	48
Salad Dressing	
Aphrodite's	214
Olive Oil	227
SALT	228
Sandwich Spread, Walnut	119
Sauces	
Cheese	179
Christmas Pudding	69
Egg	179
Garlic	40
Lemon	91
Olive, Italiano	81
Onion	179
Mint	217
Mustard	221
Mustard for Ham	222
Raisin Cider	92
Spaghetti	201
Sweet Mustard	221
White Sauce	179
Wine	43
Scrambled Eggs with Brains	17
Sea Foods	
Almond-Tuna Casserole	102
Baked Fish	22
Fish de Medici	213
Fish of Galilee	21
Jellied Tuna-Cucumber	48
Shrimp Espanol	189
Simon Peter Fish Stew	23
Sole Veronique	73
Tuna-Noodle Casserole	48
Tuna Timbales	47
Seraphim Pudding	197
Shrimp Espanol	189
Sinuhe Salad	27
Simon Peter Fish Stew	23

Sole Veronique	73
Solomon's Cinnamon Cantaloupe	193
Solomon's Gold, Apricots	57
Soup	
Barley Barzillai	106
Cream of Cucumber	139
Leek	156
Lehi Lentils	115
Sultan's, Pomegranate	87
SUGARCANE	233
Flower Petal Preserves	236
Molasses Cake	237

t

Tadmor Delight	66
Tamarah Pie	65
TUNA	45
Almond-Tuna Casserole	102
Cucumber-Tuna Salad	48
Noodle-Tuna Casserole	48
Timbales	47

u

Veal Kidney Chops	30
Vegetables (see by Name)	
Vine and Sea Salad	74
VINEGAR	238
Candy Vinaigrette	242
Liver Vinaigrette	40
Pot Roast Vinaigrette	241
Vinegar Pie	240
Vinegar Taffy	242

w

WALNUTS	116
Chicken with Walnuts	119
King Solomon's Nut Loaf	118
Sandwich Spread	119
WATERMELON	93
Crazy Candy	96
Pharaoh's Fruit Bowl	95
Rind Pickles	95
WHEAT	120
Bulgur, How to Cook	122
Wheat-Berry Cereal	124
Wheat-Meat Loaf	123
Wheaten Stuffing	123
White Sauce	179
WINE	243
Custard	244
Rabbit in Wine Sauce	43
Roast Leg of Lamb	34
Roman Punch	245
Wassail Bowl	246

y

YOGURT	180
Beef Yoganoff	183
Lemon Cake	184